Series Titles

EARLY MEDIEVAL TIMES
was created and produced by McRae Books Srl
Via del Salviatino, 1 — 50016 — Fiesole
(Florence), (Italy)
info@mcraebooks.com
www.mcraebooks.com

Publishers: Anne McRae, Marco Nardi
Series Editor: Anne McRae
Author: John Malam
Main Illustrations: Francesca D'Ottavi pp. 18–19,
28–29; Giacinto Gaudenzi 20–21, 40–41; Magicgroup,
Sro. p. 24–25; MM comunicazione (Manuela Cappon,
Monica Favilli) pp. 16–17, 34–35; Sabrina Marconi p.
13; Tiziano Perotto 26–27; Claudia Saraceni pp.
22–23; Sergio pp. 14–15, 30–31, 32–33, 36–37

Illustrations: Studio Stalio (Alessandro Cantucci,
Fabiano Fabbrucci)
Maps: M. Paola Baldanzi
Photos: Bibliothèque nationale de France p. 43;
Bridgeman Art Library, London/Alinari Photo Library,
Florence pp. 38bl, 44–45; Scala Archives, Florence pp.
7b, 10–11b
Art Director: Marco Nardi
Layouts: Starry Dogs Books Ltd.
Project Editor: Loredana Agosta
Research: Ellie Smith, Loredana Agosta
Editing: Tall Tree Ltd, London
Repro: Litocolor, Florence

Consultant:
Dr. Scott Ashley, Lecturer in Medieval History at the
University of Newcastle upon Tyne. He is interested
in the history of Europe from the end of the western
Roman Empire to the 12th century, and especially in
the Carolingian empire, Anglo-Saxon England and the
Vikings. He is currently writing a global history of
the Vikings.

Library of Congress Cataloging-in-Publication Data

Malam, John, 1957-
  Early medieval times / John Malam.
      p. cm. -- (History of the world ; 8)
  Includes index.
  Summary: "A detailed overview of the history in
Europe from the collapse of the Roman Empire in
western Europe in the late 400s to the Norman
conquest of England in 1066"--Provided by publisher.
  ISBN 978-8860981509
  1. Middle Ages--Juvenile literature. 2. Europe--
History--476-1492--Juvenile literature. 3. Civilization,
Medieval--Juvenile literature. I. Title.
  D121.M33 2009
  940.1'4--dc22
                                        2008008405

Printed and bound in Malaysia.

HISTORY

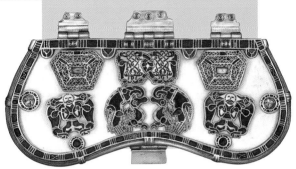

Early Medieval Times

John Malam

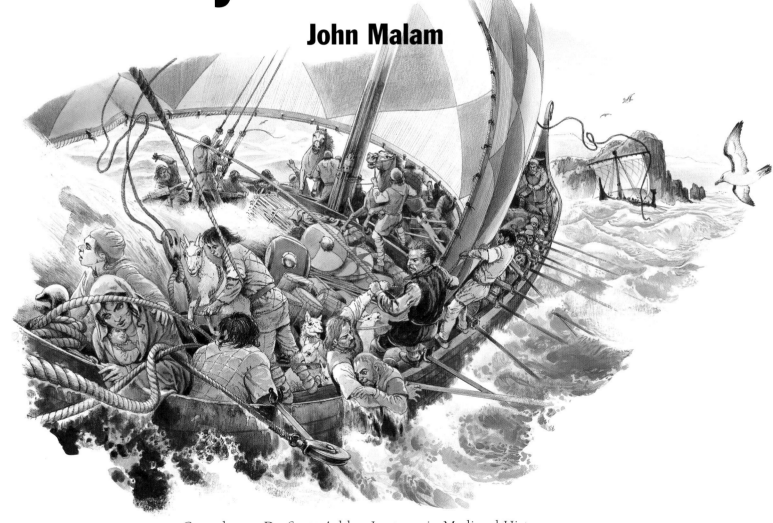

Consultant: Dr. Scott Ashley, Lecturer in Medieval History
at the University of Newcastle upon Tyne

Zak BOOKS

Contents

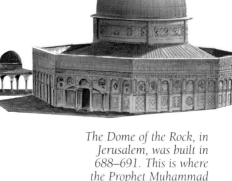

The Dome of the Rock, in Jerusalem, was built in 688–691. This is where the Prophet Muhammad is believed to have ascended into heaven. It is one of the holiest sites of the Muslim faith.

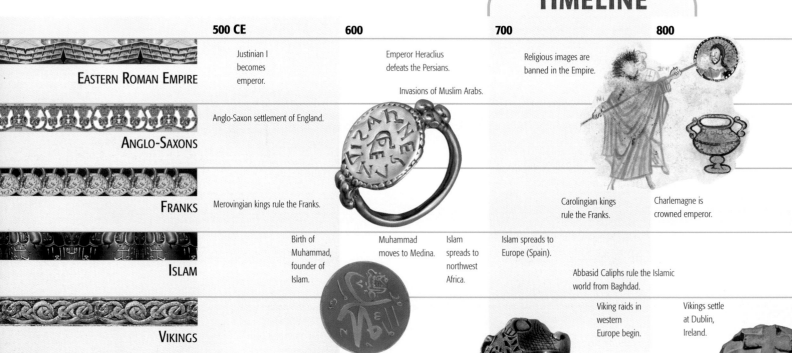

TIMELINE

	500 CE	600	700	800
EASTERN ROMAN EMPIRE	Justinian I becomes emperor.	Emperor Heraclius defeats the Persians. Invasions of Muslim Arabs.	Religious images are banned in the Empire.	
ANGLO-SAXONS	Anglo-Saxon settlement of England.			
FRANKS	Merovingian kings rule the Franks.		Carolingian kings rule the Franks.	Charlemagne is crowned emperor.
ISLAM		Birth of Muhammad, founder of Islam. Muhammad moves to Medina. Islam spreads to northwest Africa.	Islam spreads to Europe (Spain). Abbasid Caliphs rule the Islamic world from Baghdad.	
VIKINGS			Viking raids in western Europe begin.	Vikings settle at Dublin, Ireland.
RUSSIA AND EASTERN EUROPE		The Slavs conquer the Balkan region of eastern Europe.		The Great Moravian State flourishes in central Europe.
HOLY ROMAN EMPIRE AND THE CHURCH	Monasticism spreads to western Europe.		The Franks give the pope lands in central Italy.	

Introduction

This volume covers 600 years of history, from the late 400s to about 1000. It begins with the collapse of the Roman Empire in western Europe and ends with the Norman conquest of England in 1066. This was a period when the ancient world ended and the Middle Ages began. The changeover began while the Romans still controlled much of western Europe. Starting in the late 300s, large groups of displaced Germanic peoples—Saxons, Franks, Visigoths, Ostrogoths, Lombards, and others—migrated into the Roman Empire, signaling a slow end to Roman domination. They carved up the Roman world between them and created their own kingdoms. But Rome did not disappear without trace. To the east, the city of Constantinople (present-day Istanbul in Turkey) became the vibrant center of the Eastern Roman, or Byzantine, Empire. Also during this period the religion of Islam was founded by the Prophet Muhammad in Arabia. It was a time when cultures clashed, when old religions faded and new ones were accepted, when invaders became settlers and raiders became traders, and when, more than anything else, some of Europe's modern nations were born.

A glass cup in the shape of a horn. It was made in Italy in the late 500s, and may have been passed around at a feast.

This small bronze figure of Charlemagne or Charles the Bald, wearing the king's crown, was made in the 800s.

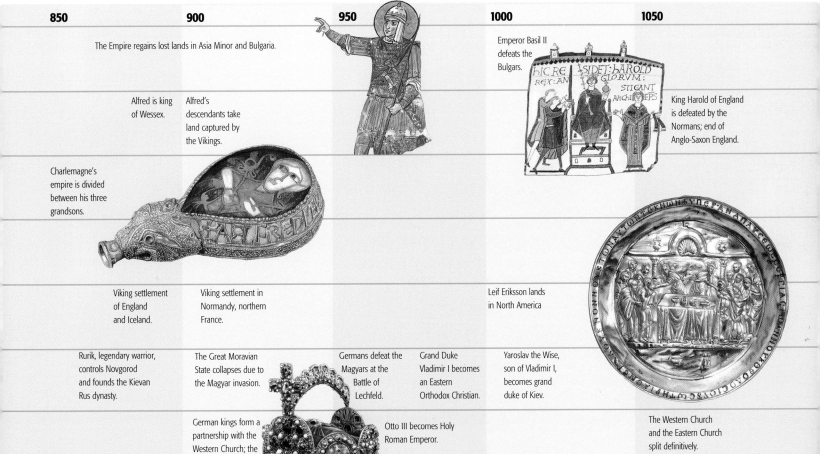

The Empire regains lost lands in Asia Minor and Bulgaria.

Alfred is king of Wessex. Alfred's descendants take land captured by the Vikings.

Emperor Basil II defeats the Bulgars.

King Harold of England is defeated by the Normans; end of Anglo-Saxon England.

Charlemagne's empire is divided between his three grandsons.

Viking settlement of England and Iceland.

Viking settlement in Normandy, northern France.

Leif Eriksson lands in North America

Rurik, legendary warrior, controls Novgorod and founds the Kievan Rus dynasty.

The Great Moravian State collapses due to the Magyar invasion.

Germans defeat the Magyars at the Battle of Lechfeld.

Grand Duke Vladimir I becomes an Eastern Orthodox Christian.

Yaroslav the Wise, son of Vladimir I, becomes grand duke of Kiev.

German kings form a partnership with the Western Church; the Holy Roman Empire is founded.

Otto III becomes Holy Roman Emperor.

The Western Church and the Eastern Church split definitively.

Western Europe in 500

The 6th century was an unsettled time in western Europe. It was the start of a period once called the Dark Ages, but which today is known as the Early Middle Ages. It was when power shifted from the Romans to Germanic peoples of north and east Europe. The Romans called them "barbarians." In 476, Rome's last emperor was deposed, leaving Germanic peoples as the region's new masters.

An armed Saxon warrior on horseback.

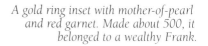

A gold ring inset with mother-of-pearl and red garnet. Made about 500, it belonged to a wealthy Frank.

Anglo-Saxons in England

Angles, Saxons, Frisians, and Jutes crossed the sea to Britain from Europe as early as the 4th century. Full-scale migrations began in c. 450 and continued until the 600s. At first there was conflict with the Britons, but when resistance faded, and Anglo-Saxon kingdoms emerged. From these kingdoms grew a country which the Anglo-Saxons called "England."

Ostrogoths in Italy

The Ostrogoths (East Goths) settled in Pannonia (present-day Hungary) in c. 450. Led by Theodoric (c. 455–526), they later invaded Italy in 488. This led to conflict with Odoacer (c. 433–493), who had deposed Rome's last emperor and become Italy's first Germanic king. Theodoric killed Odoacer, and from 493 was sole ruler of the Ostrogoth kingdom of Italy. Theodoric was a follower of Arianism, a Christian sect founded in the 4th century. He was also tolerant of other religions.

Franks in Gaul

Originally from an area east of the Rhine River, in present-day Germany, the Franks were a group of Germanic tribes. During the 300s and 400s they crossed the Rhine and raided the Roman Empire. As Roman control of northern Gaul (France and Belgium) declined, the Franks settled there, where they created a Christian kingdom.

Theodoric, the Ostrogoth leader, was buried in this tomb at Ravenna in northeast Italy.

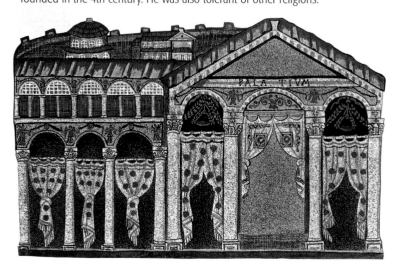

Ravenna was the Ostrogoth capital of Italy. Its churches were decorated with mosaics, like this one (left).

Visigoths in Iberia

In the 370s the Goths of eastern Europe divided into Ostrogoths (East Goths) and Visigoths (West Goths), and a time of migration followed. The Visigoths moved west into the Roman Empire and in 410 they sacked Rome. Unable to settle in Italy, they moved to Iberia (Spain and Portugal) where they created a Christian kingdom.

This ornate belt buckle was probably worn by a rich Visigoth in the 500s.

GERMANIC PEOPLES IN EUROPE

Burgundians
Byzantium
Franks
Ostrogoths
Vandals
Visigoths

RHEIMS
PARIS • TRIER
BORDEAUX
MARSEILLE • RAVENNA
TOLEDO
ROME
CORDOBA
CONSTANTINOPLE
CARTHAGE • ATHENS
MEDITERRANEAN SEA

Divided Kingdoms

Western Europe in the Early Middle Ages was a region divided into kingdoms formed by groups of Germanic peoples. They settled in areas once part of the Roman Empire, and as their kingdoms became established, the borders of recognizable present-day countries slowly evolved from them.

This mosaic comes from the Baptistery of the Arians, built in Ravenna during the time of Theodoric. It shows the baptism of Christ (in the center).

KINGDOMS EMERGE

c. 450
Angles, Saxons, Frisians, and Jutes begin to migrate to Britain and form kingdoms.

400s
Franks establish a kingdom in Gaul.

410
Visigoths briefly seize Rome.

476
The Roman Empire in the west ends when the last emperor, Romulus Augustulus, is deposed by Germanic invaders.

488
Ostrogoths invade Italy and create a kingdom.

507
Franks defeat Visigoths and drive them into Spain and Portugal where they form a kingdom.

The Spread of Christianity

Once outlawed by the Romans, Christianity became Rome's state religion under Constantine in 313. As missionaries spread the Christian message, people abandoned their pagan beliefs and were converted through baptism to the faith. However, Christianity was slow to spread, and it was not until the 1100s that the last of western Europe's pagans, the Swedish Vikings, finally gave up their old religion.

Right: A decorated letter from the Book of Kells (the Gospels in Latin). It was created in c. 800 by Celtic monks of Ireland or Scotland.

A Christian Way of Life

A way of life for Christian communities emerged in the Eastern Roman Empire in the 300s. Known as monasticism, it was practised by men (monks) or women (nuns) who dedicated their lives to God. At first they lived as hermits in isolated places, but by the 500s monasticism had spread to western Europe.

Christian Art and the Power of Images

Art played a major role in the spread of early Christianity. It was a means of visual communication, through which powerful images transmitted the ideas and beliefs of Christians. The cross on which Christ died became Christianity's international symbol. Wherever the religion was accepted, a distinctive style of Christian art developed.

A person showed their belief in Christ by being baptized. They were dipped in water to wash away their former lives, after which they began new lives as Christians. Baptism was the method of conversion to Christianity.

Left: In Britain and Ireland, intricately carved stone crosses appeared from the 600s. Some were memorials to the dead, others marked preaching sites.

A Viking mold, used to make Christian crosses and pagan Thor's hammers (center).

Missionary Monks and Nuns

Monks lived and worked in monasteries, nuns in convents. They belonged to religious Orders (families), such as the Benedictines for monks (founded in Italy in 529 by St. Benedict), and the Carmelites for nuns (founded in Palestine, c. 1170). Missionary monks and nuns were sent to live and work among pagans, as St. Augustine of Canterbury (died c. 605) did when he and his fellow Benedictines arrived in England in 597. Christianity spread through their teaching.

Augustine was sent to Britain by Pope Gregory I. Canterbury, the capital of the kingdom of Kent, became the center of Christianity in Britain.

Benedictine monks offer a book to the abbot of their monastery.

The Work of Monks

In the Early Middle Ages, writing was the work of monks. They worked in monasteries, mainly copying out the Bible. They wrote on sheets of parchment (sheepskin or goatskin) or vellum (calfskin). In the centuries before the printing press came into use, all books were handwritten. By the 600s books were being made with brightly colored letters and pictures, known today as "illuminated manuscripts."

St. Columba (521–597), an Irish missionary, sailed to Scotland in 563 together with his companions. They landed at Iona and went about converting the Picts (Scottish Celts).

THE SPREAD OF CHRISTIANITY

IONA
LINDISFARNE
YORK
TINTAGEL
CANTERBURY
ST BRIEUC
ROUEN
SOISSONS
LIGUGE
BREGENZ
MILAN
AUILEIA
ZARAGOZA
NURSIA
BLACK SEA
MARSEILLES
CONSTANTINOPLE
TOLEDO
ROME
VIVARIUM
HIPPO REGIUS
ST LATMOS
MEDITERRANEAN SEA
JERUSALEM
ALEXANDRIA
THEBES

The Monastic World

This map shows how monasticism emerged from Egypt in the 4th century, spreading Christianity across Europe. The first monks were hermits, living piously in the deserts, but in time they lived communally, following the rules of their Order.

- Benedictine monasticism
- Celtic monasticism
- Eastern-inspired monasticism
- Route of monastic expansion
- Monastery

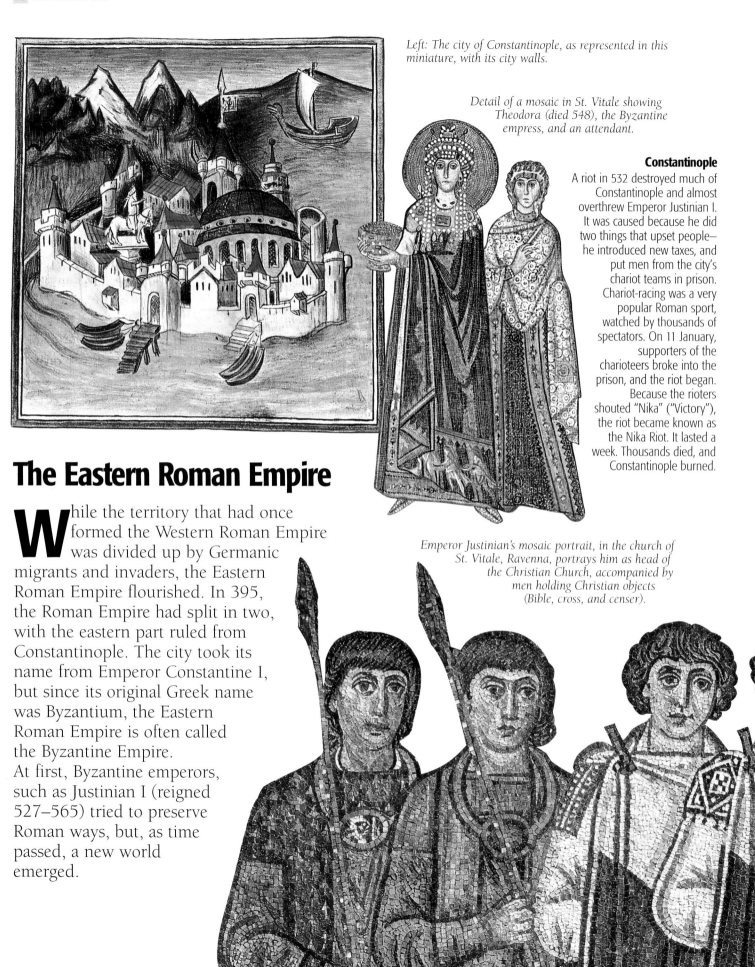

Left: The city of Constantinople, as represented in this miniature, with its city walls.

Detail of a mosaic in St. Vitale showing Theodora (died 548), the Byzantine empress, and an attendant.

Constantinople

A riot in 532 destroyed much of Constantinople and almost overthrew Emperor Justinian I. It was caused because he did two things that upset people— he introduced new taxes, and put men from the city's chariot teams in prison. Chariot-racing was a very popular Roman sport, watched by thousands of spectators. On 11 January, supporters of the charioteers broke into the prison, and the riot began. Because the rioters shouted "Nika" ("Victory"), the riot became known as the Nika Riot. It lasted a week. Thousands died, and Constantinople burned.

The Eastern Roman Empire

While the territory that had once formed the Western Roman Empire was divided up by Germanic migrants and invaders, the Eastern Roman Empire flourished. In 395, the Roman Empire had split in two, with the eastern part ruled from Constantinople. The city took its name from Emperor Constantine I, but since its original Greek name was Byzantium, the Eastern Roman Empire is often called the Byzantine Empire.

At first, Byzantine emperors, such as Justinian I (reigned 527–565) tried to preserve Roman ways, but, as time passed, a new world emerged.

Emperor Justinian's mosaic portrait, in the church of St. Vitale, Ravenna, portrays him as head of the Christian Church, accompanied by men holding Christian objects (Bible, cross, and censer).

THE EASTERN ROMAN EMPIRE

RAVENNA

BLACK SEA

ROME
CONSTANTINOPLE
NICEA

ATHENS
ANTIOCH

MEDITERRANEAN SEA

Byzantine Empire, 1204

Byzantine Empire, 1025

Byzantine Empire, 628

The Empire Expands, then Shrinks
Under Emperor Justinian I, the Byzantine Empire expanded to the west, absorbing territories in southern Europe and North Africa that had once been part of the Roman Empire. By 1025 (when Emperor Basil II died), the Empire had shrunk back to its homeland of eastern Europe and Asia Minor.

Emperor Justinian's Law Code
In 528, Emperor Justinian I ordered a group of leading officials to gather together all the laws of the Roman world. It took 14 months to compile the laws, and in 529 Justinian's Code was published in 12 books, containing more than one million words. Justinian wanted his law code to become widely used so that Roman influence would spread far. This worked, and from the 11th century onward his code became the basis of western Europe's legal system.

Justinian's Code, written in Latin, was a great feat of organization. It made Roman law highly logical. This page was printed in 1512.

BYZANTINES

330
The capital of the Roman Empire is moved to Constantinople.

523
Emperor Justinian I marries Theodora.

532
The general Belisarius (c. 505–565) suppresses the Nika Riot. Later, in 533–534, he defeats the Vandals of Africa.

610–641
The reign of Emperor Heraclius who defeats the Persians.

634–642
Invasions of Muslim Arabs.

730–843
Religious images are banned in the Empire.

867–1025
The Empire regains lost lands in Asia Minor and Bulgaria.

1014
Emperor Basil II defeats the Bulgars.

1025
Emperor Basil II dies. During the next 56 years 13 different rulers take the throne.

Byzantine Art and Culture

Constantinople was at the heart of the Byzantine Empire—one of the great medieval empires. The Byzantines created a distinctive Greek-speaking, Christian culture that lasted for a thousand years in eastern Europe and Asia Minor (Turkey). Their world survived until 1453, when Constantinople was captured by Ottoman Turks, who were Muslims, and the Byzantine Empire was brought to an end.

The Eastern Church

Over time, a schism, or split, developed in the Christian Church, dividing it into the Eastern Orthodox Church (centered on Constantinople) and the Western Roman Church (centered on Rome). While the Eastern Church argued about the meaning of the Bible's instructions, such as whether icons were idolatrous or not, the Western Church remained calm. The two Churches continued to grow apart, with the Eastern Church refusing to accept the authority of the pope.

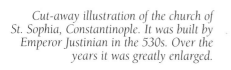

Cut-away illustration of the church of St. Sophia, Constantinople. It was built by Emperor Justinian in the 530s. Over the years it was greatly enlarged.

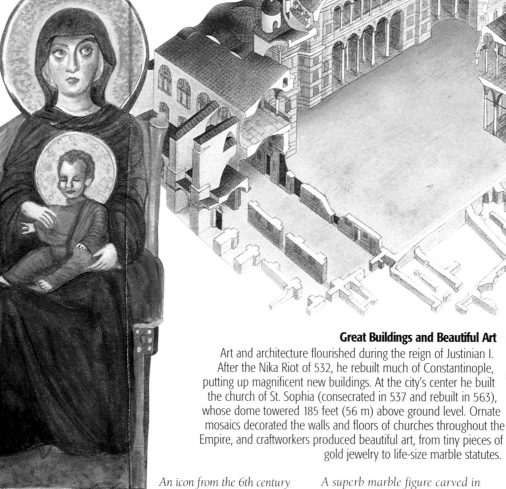

Great Buildings and Beautiful Art

Art and architecture flourished during the reign of Justinian I. After the Nika Riot of 532, he rebuilt much of Constantinople, putting up magnificent new buildings. At the city's center he built the church of St. Sophia (consecrated in 537 and rebuilt in 563), whose dome towered 185 feet (56 m) above ground level. Ornate mosaics decorated the walls and floors of churches throughout the Empire, and craftworkers produced beautiful art, from tiny pieces of gold jewelry to life-size marble statutes.

An icon from the 6th century showing the Virgin Mary and the Christ child. Icons were popular in the East.

A superb marble figure carved in Constantinople in the early 500s. The woman holds a scroll, a sign she was well educated.

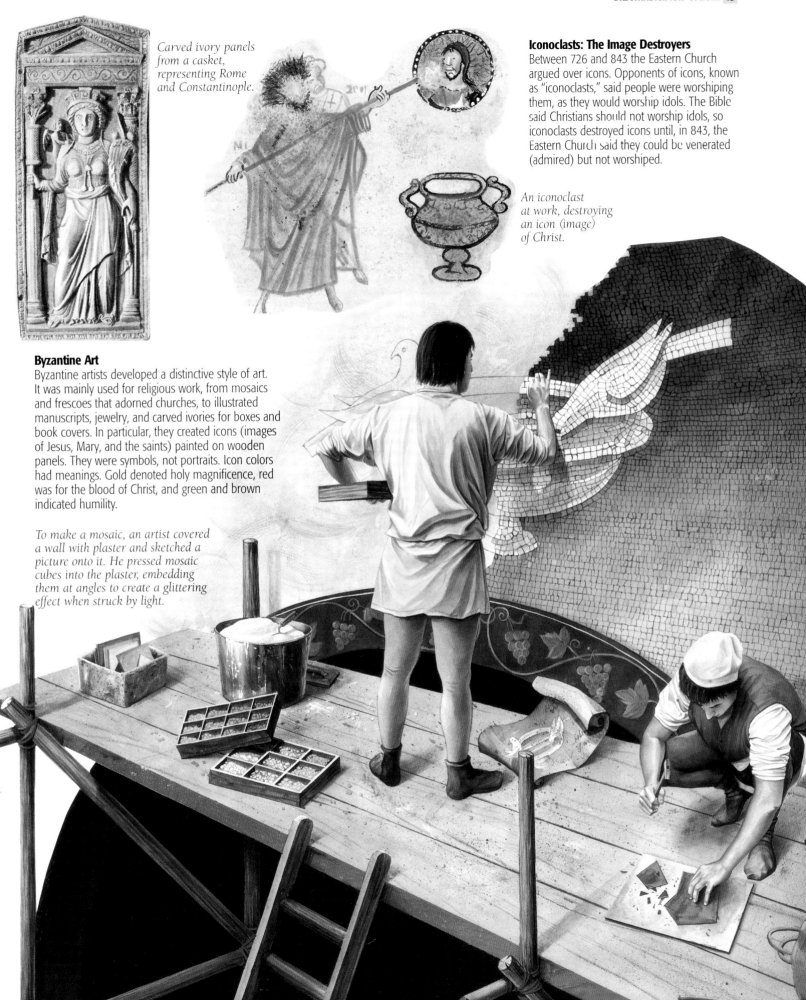

Carved ivory panels from a casket, representing Rome and Constantinople.

Iconoclasts: The Image Destroyers

Between 726 and 843 the Eastern Church argued over icons. Opponents of icons, known as "iconoclasts," said people were worshiping them, as they would worship idols. The Bible said Christians should not worship idols, so iconoclasts destroyed icons until, in 843, the Eastern Church said they could be venerated (admired) but not worshiped.

An iconoclast at work, destroying an icon (image) of Christ.

Byzantine Art

Byzantine artists developed a distinctive style of art. It was mainly used for religious work, from mosaics and frescoes that adorned churches, to illustrated manuscripts, jewelry, and carved ivories for boxes and book covers. In particular, they created icons (images of Jesus, Mary, and the saints) painted on wooden panels. They were symbols, not portraits. Icon colors had meanings. Gold denoted holy magnificence, red was for the blood of Christ, and green and brown indicated humility.

To make a mosaic, an artist covered a wall with plaster and sketched a picture onto it. He pressed mosaic cubes into the plaster, embedding them at angles to create a glittering effect when struck by light.

Mosaic from Carthage, North Africa, of a Vandal horseman. Roman crafts, such as mosaic-making, continued under the Vandals.

The Visigoths had commercial contacts throughout the Mediterranean. This Visigothic brass pendant with beasts, dating from 500–600, shows artistic influence from Greece and the Near East.

Visigoths in Spain

From Italy in the 400s, the Visigoths moved to southern France and northern Spain. But in the early 500s conflict with the Franks forced them out of France. They made Iberia (Spain and Portugal) their kingdom, with Toledo as the capital. In 711, Muslims from North Africa invaded, and the Visigoths ceased to exist.

Vandals in North Africa

The Vandals, from the north of Europe, migrated further than any other Germanic people. In 406, they moved through France and into Spain. But, in 429, the Visigoths, who also had their sights on Spain, forced the Vandals to cross to North Africa, where they built a kingdom. In 533, an army from the Eastern Roman Empire defeated the Vandals, and their kingdom ended.

A Lombard brooch made in about 600. In the center is a Roman cameo—already 300 years old when the Lombard jeweler reused it.

Italy and the Lombards

The Lombards, from Sweden, crossed the Alps in 568 and formed a kingdom in northern Italy. In the 750s they tried to capture Rome—home of the pope, head of the Roman Church. He asked the Franks for help. In 774, the Franks defeated the Lombards and their kingdom was split into small states.

The Mediterranean World

The map of Europe changed considerably between 500 and 800. Around the Mediterranean, Ostrogoths, Visigoths, Vandals, and Lombards created short-lived kingdoms within the remains of the collapsed Western Roman Empire. Attempts were made by Eastern Romans, and other groups, to defeat the "barbarian" kingdoms, and some areas of land changed hands many times.

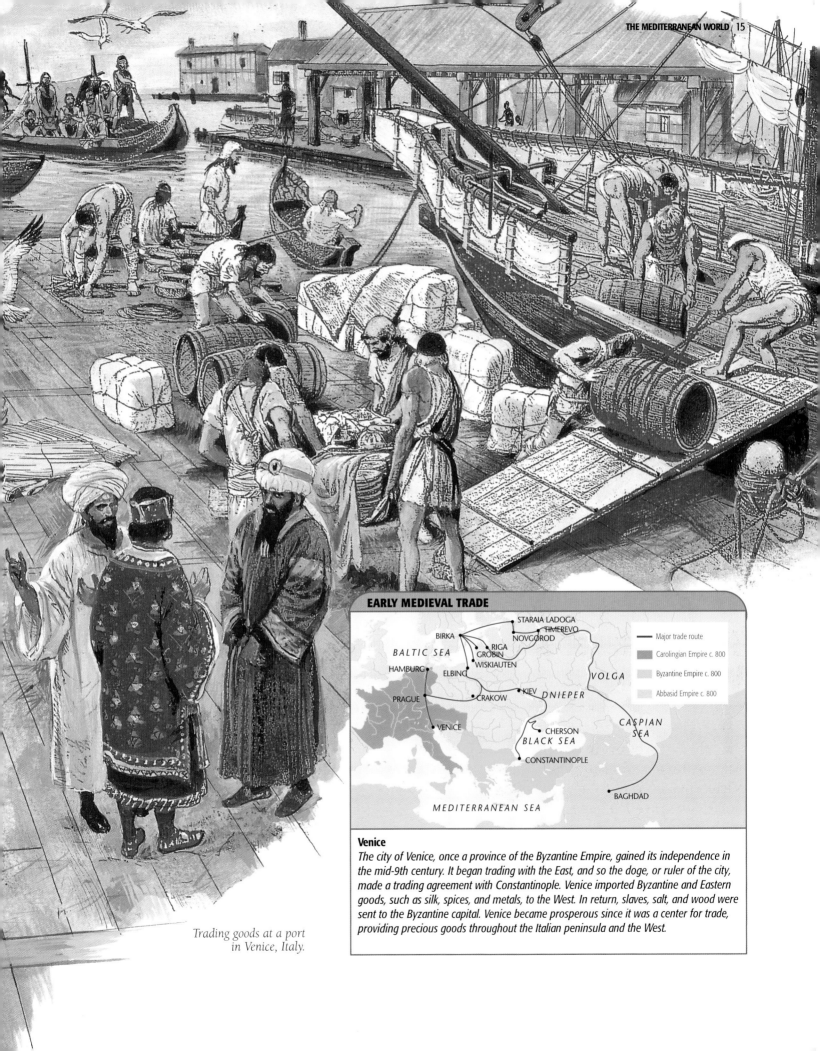

EARLY MEDIEVAL TRADE

STARAIA LADOGA
TIMEREVO
BIRKA
NOVGOROD
RIGA
GROBIN
BALTIC SEA
WISKIAUTEN
HAMBURG
ELBING
VOLGA
PRAGUE
CRAKOW
KIEV
DNIEPER
VENICE
CASPIAN SEA
CHERSON
BLACK SEA
CONSTANTINOPLE
BAGHDAD
MEDITERRANEAN SEA

— Major trade route

Carolingian Empire c. 800

Byzantine Empire c. 800

Abbasid Empire c. 800

Venice

The city of Venice, once a province of the Byzantine Empire, gained its independence in the mid-9th century. It began trading with the East, and so the doge, or ruler of the city, made a trading agreement with Constantinople. Venice imported Byzantine and Eastern goods, such as silk, spices, and metals, to the West. In return, slaves, salt, and wood were sent to the Byzantine capital. Venice became prosperous since it was a center for trade, providing precious goods throughout the Italian peninsula and the West.

Trading goods at a port in Venice, Italy.

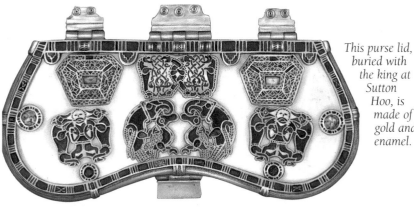

This purse lid, buried with the king at Sutton Hoo, is made of gold and enamel.

ANGLO-SAXON SETTLEMENT OF BRITAIN

→ Angles
→ Saxons
■ Non-Romanised
■ Romanised

HIGHLANDS

IRELAND

NORTH SEA

NORTHUMBRIA

MERCIA   EAST ANGLIA

ESSEX
WESSEX SUSSEX
KENT

King Alfred the Great

Alfred (849–899) is the most famous of the early kings of England. In 871, his kingdom of Wessex was attacked by Vikings, and Alfred led an army against them. He fought the Vikings for years, and in 886 took London from them. After that the Vikings stayed in the north, while the south of England came under Anglo-Saxon control, with Alfred as its king.

Burial Place of Kings

The first kings of the Anglo-Saxon kingdom of East Anglia appear to have been buried at Sutton Hoo, Suffolk. One of them may have been King Raedwald (died c. 625). He is thought to have been buried inside the largest mound at Sutton Hoo, which contained a wooden ship 98 feet (30 m) in length. His body was in the middle of the ship, surrounded by a rich collection of grave goods, including Swedish-style weapons and helmets, gold and silver jewelry, gold coins from France, and silver cups.

Anglo-Saxon Kingdoms

Most Anglo-Saxons arrived in Britain between 450 and 650 and at first settled in the east and south-east. By the 600s southern Britain was divided into the Anglo-Saxon kingdoms of Northumbria, East Anglia, Mercia, Kent, Sussex, Essex, and Wessex. The kingdoms were rivals, but by the 960s they had merged to create the nation of England.

The Alfred Jewel, which dates from the reign of King Alfred the Great, is made of gold, cloisonne enamel, and rock crystal. It bears the inscription "Alfred ordered me to be made."

The burial of an Anglo-Saxon king at Sutton Hoo. He lay inside a chamber built on a ship, which was then covered by a mound of earth.

The Anglo-Saxons

I n 401 and 402 Roman troops were withdrawn from Britain to defend Italy from Germanic invaders. Then, in 410, the Romans abandoned Britain completely, leaving its towns to look after themselves. At the same time, Germanic peoples from northern Germany and Scandinavia (Angles, Saxons, Frisians, and Jutes) crossed the sea and began to settle in eastern and southern Britain. They came to be known as Anglo-Saxons, and they created a country called England. The Anglo-Saxon period lasted for 600 years, from 410 to 1066.

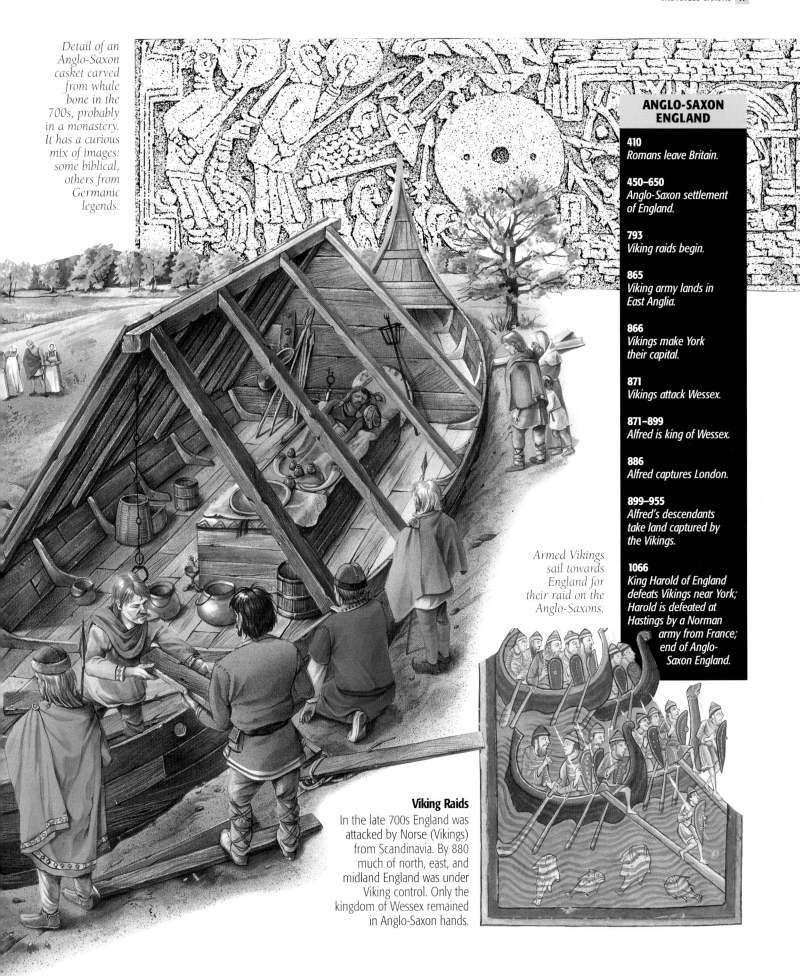

Detail of an Anglo-Saxon casket carved from whale bone in the 700s, probably in a monastery. It has a curious mix of images: some biblical, others from Germanic legends.

ANGLO-SAXON ENGLAND

410
Romans leave Britain.

450–650
Anglo-Saxon settlement of England.

793
Viking raids begin.

865
Viking army lands in East Anglia.

866
Vikings make York their capital.

871
Vikings attack Wessex.

871–899
Alfred is king of Wessex.

886
Alfred captures London.

899–955
Alfred's descendants take land captured by the Vikings.

1066
King Harold of England defeats Vikings near York; Harold is defeated at Hastings by a Norman army from France; end of Anglo-Saxon England.

Armed Vikings sail towards England for their raid on the Anglo-Saxons.

Viking Raids
In the late 700s England was attacked by Norse (Vikings) from Scandinavia. By 880 much of north, east, and midland England was under Viking control. Only the kingdom of Wessex remained in Anglo-Saxon hands.

The Franks

The Franks were one of western Europe's most successful groups during the Early Middle Ages. Their rise to power began in the early 400s, when they moved to the northern part of France and Belgium. Following the collapse of the Roman Empire, the Franks quickly became masters of most of France in the early 500s. They went on to create a vast Christian empire that, later in the 800s, stretched from France in the west to Hungary in the east.

THE FRANKS

460s–751
Merovingian kings rule the Franks.

751–911
Carolingian kings rule the Franks.

771
Charlemagne becomes sole ruler of the Franks; begins to create a Christian empire.

800
Charlemagne is crowned Emperor of the Romans, a title suggesting he has revived the western half of the former Roman Empire, with him at its head.

814
Charlemagne dies.

843
Charlemagne's empire is divided among his three grandsons.

Glass Cups for the Rich

Most craft industries went into decline after the end of the Roman period. However, Frankish craftworkers kept the art of glassmaking alive. Their most notable vessel is known as a "claw beaker," after the "claws" of glass on the outside. Only the wealthiest Franks could have afforded such luxurious drinking cups, and to own one would have been a sign of a person's high-standing. When a person died, their glass beaker might be buried with them.

Early Kings of the Franks

The early kings of the Franks are known as the Merovingians, named after Merovech, the legendary Frankish king (reigned 447–458?). He founded a dynasty that ruled for some 300 years. One of his descendants was Clovis (reigned 481–511), who made Christianity the official religion. By the 700s the Merovingians had become weak. In 751, a new dynasty of Frankish kings seized power under Pepin III (reigned 751–768). These rulers are known as the Carolingians, after Charlemagne, their most famous king.

A Frankish glass claw beaker made in the late 400s. This one, made in northern Europe, was discovered in a grave in the north of England.

A Queen of the Franks

Excavations in Paris, France, uncovered the burial of a woman from the early Frankish royal family. Her finger-ring had the name "Arnegunde" on it. Queen Arnegunde was married to a king of the Franks. She died in about 570. Arnegunde had been buried in a luxurious dress made from silk, decorated with gold thread. She wore gold earrings and other pieces of expensive jewelry.

The gold ring of Queen Arnegunde.

These are the remains of Queen Arnegunde. Her dress had been made from Chinese silk.

Queen Radegund (518–587), pictured feeding the poor in this detail from a miniature, established an abbey at Poitiers. She got the Merovingian kings to foster the monastic movement.

DIVISION OF FRANKISH POWER, 561

TOURNAI

SOISSONS
PARIS · RHEIMS · METZ

ORLÉANS ·

AUSTRASIA

· CHALON

NEUSTRIA BURGUNDY EASTERN ROMAN EMPIRE

AUVERGNE

The Frankish Kingdoms
From the 6th to the 9th century the Empire grew to include most of France, the Low Countries, Germany west of the Elbe, Austria, Switzerland, and part of Italy. The Merovingian Empire was divided into several kingdoms—Neustria in the west, Austrasia in the east, and Burgundy in the south. During this period there were constant battles among the kingdoms' rulers.

- Charibert
- Chilperic
- ···· Territory of Frankish overlordship
- Guntram
- ● Royal residence
- Sigebert

Clovis, king of the Franks, was born a pagan but converted to the Christian faith, setting an example for others to follow. He was baptized during the later years of his reign.

Charlemagne, Emperor of the West

When Charles became sole ruler of the Franks in 771, he was determined to enlarge his kingdom, unite Europe under his rule, and spread Christianity. Over the next 30 years he conquered lands, converted pagans, and created a vast Christian empire over a large part of western Europe. For this, he became known as Charlemagne, or Charles the Great, and the pope made him Emperor of the Romans. During his reign, religion, learning, law, and the arts flourished.

During his reign, Charlemagne fostered schools and libraries. Many of these became centers of manuscript illumination, called scriptoria. *This illuminated page, showing St. Luke, is from one of the Golden Gospels which was written in the school of Aachen.*

Aachen, Center of Learning

Charlemagne's capital was at Aachen, which today is on the borders of Germany, Belgium, and the Netherlands. Because he wanted the city to be as grand as Rome in the days of the Roman Empire, its buildings were planned on a large scale. His palace at Aachen became a center of learning, where scholars studied Roman texts, rediscovering "lost" knowledge from the past.

MAVRVS·ALBINVS· SISMAR...INVS

Alcuin (c. 740–804), seen here sharing his knowledge with others, was an English scholar from York who settled in Aachen, where he became head of the palace school. He worked as Charlemagne's teacher and political adviser.

The Western Christian Empire

Charlemagne's empire was created by force. During his 40-year reign he organized about 60 military campaigns in which his armies of Franks defeated other Germanic peoples. He conquered the Saxons of northern Europe and the Lombards of Italy. In the north of Spain he created a zone that separated his territory from the Muslim empire of Islam.

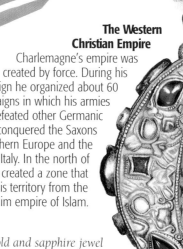

This gold and sapphire jewel was made in Charlemagne's lifetime. It is said to hold a piece of Christ's Cross.

Emperor of the West

On Christmas day 800, Pope Leo III crowned Charlemagne Emperor of the Romans—the first western ruler in 300 years to be called "emperor." It put Charlemagne on equal terms with the emperor of the Byzantine Empire that lay to the east. His coronation marked the start of a new period in the history of western Europe, laying the foundations for the creation of the Holy Roman Empire in the early 900s.

The coronation of Charlemagne, in St. Peter's Church, Rome. He came to be regarded as the first Holy Roman Emperor.

Outside Threats

The empire of Charlemagne was short-lived. Within 30 years of his death it disintegrated. There were also outside threats—Magyars raided France, Germany, and Italy; Vikings attacked and settled within its borders; and Saracens crossed the Mediterranean to its southern region.

Divided Empire

Charlemagne's empire passed to his son, Louis the Pious (reigned 814–840). Louis had three sons and he wanted the eldest, Lothair, to inherit the Empire. This angered his younger sons, and fighting broke out. In 843, the brothers split the empire in three. Charles the Bald took the western part (France), Lothair the center (from the North Sea to northern Italy), and Louis the German the eastern part (Germany).

Emperor Lothair I (795–855), grandson of Charlemagne.

Everyday Life

In a time long before intensive farming methods, food was produced on a small scale by families for their own consumption. Villages centered around farmers' fields and peasant farmers spent most of the day working the land. Besides farming, Early Medieval village-dwellers also worked at other necessary chores. Women wove all the cloth, using wool from the sheep raised on the farm. Metalsmiths made iron tools while craftworkers made fine metal objects in distinctive Medieval styles.

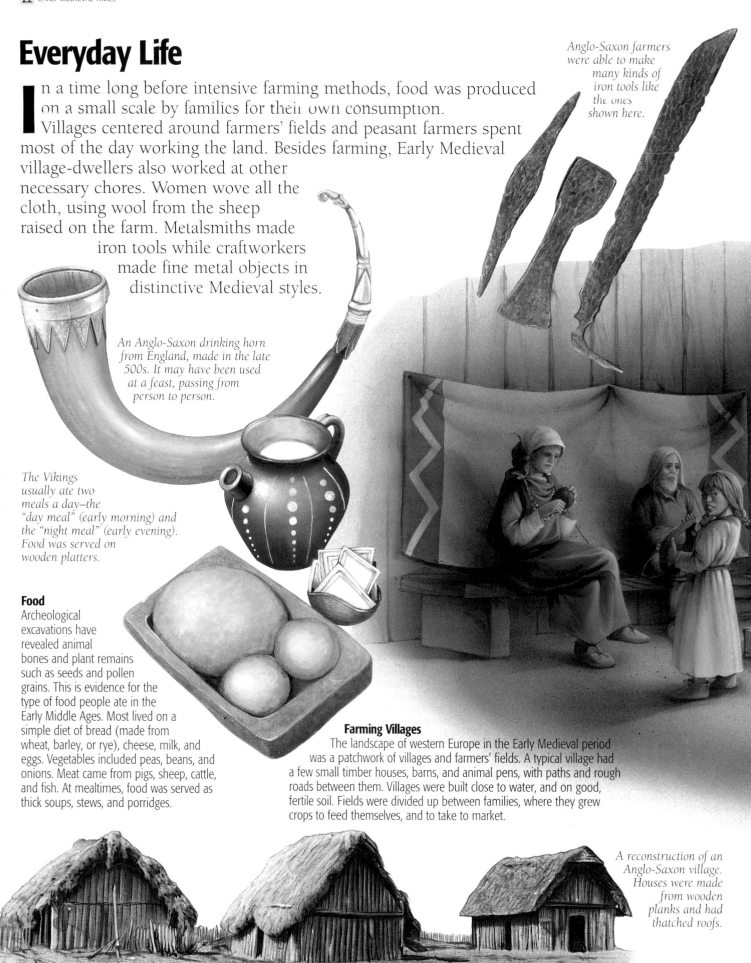

Anglo-Saxon farmers were able to make many kinds of iron tools like the ones shown here.

An Anglo-Saxon drinking horn from England, made in the late 500s. It may have been used at a feast, passing from person to person.

The Vikings usually ate two meals a day—the "day meal" (early morning) and the "night meal" (early evening). Food was served on wooden platters.

Food
Archeological excavations have revealed animal bones and plant remains such as seeds and pollen grains. This is evidence for the type of food people ate in the Early Middle Ages. Most lived on a simple diet of bread (made from wheat, barley, or rye), cheese, milk, and eggs. Vegetables included peas, beans, and onions. Meat came from pigs, sheep, cattle, and fish. At mealtimes, food was served as thick soups, stews, and porridges.

Farming Villages
The landscape of western Europe in the Early Medieval period was a patchwork of villages and farmers' fields. A typical village had a few small timber houses, barns, and animal pens, with paths and rough roads between them. Villages were built close to water, and on good, fertile soil. Fields were divided up between families, where they grew crops to feed themselves, and to take to market.

A reconstruction of an Anglo-Saxon village. Houses were made from wooden planks and had thatched roofs.

Agricultural Progress

Throughout the Early Middle Ages progress was made in agriculture. In the north of Europe, where soils were wetter and heavier, people began using stronger plows than their Roman predecessors. Their plows dug deep, enabling them to farm soils that had never been farmed before. And with more land being used for agriculture, more food could be grown. In the south of Europe, where soils were lighter and thinner, farmers continued to use light plows. By the end of the Early Middle Ages, agriculture was the main form of work for most people.

Early Medieval farmers learned how to harness several animals together, making it easier for farm equipment to be pulled and used.

Anglo-Saxon Life

After a hard day of work in the fields, the family would gather around the hearth at the center of the one-room house, where the family's food was cooked over the open fire. The Anglo-Saxons were famous for their love of alcoholic drinks. They enjoyed ale (made from cereals), beer (a sweet, strong drink, not like modern beer), mead (made from honey), and wine imported from mainland Europe. Non-alcoholic drinks included buttermilk, skimmed milk, and whey.

An elder member of the family provides entertainment with his storytelling accompanied by the music of his lute.

This brooch, found in Scotland, was made in c. 700. It shows both Irish and Anglo-Saxon influences in metalworking.

Crafts

Some crafts went into decline during the Early Medieval period. For example, between about 500 and 800 very little pottery was made in Anglo-Saxon England. Perhaps vessels of wood or leather were preferred to ones made from clay. Other crafts, such as metalwork, blossomed, creating new styles of Medieval art. Jewelers produced richly decorated brooches, belt buckles, and rings, using gold, silver, semi-precious stones, and colorful enamels.

The Birth and Rise of Islam

In the early 600s, Arabia was a region where many gods were worshiped. All this changed when the Prophet Muhammad began preaching that Allah was the one and only god. In 622, he founded a new religion called Islam, meaning "submission." Islam rapidly attracted followers, known as Muslims, and by the time of Muhammad's death, in 632, it had spread throughout Arabia.

The crescent and star is a traditional Muslim symbol, used for centuries. It is not strictly a religious or Islamic symbol, and its meaning is uncertain.

Islam's Holy Book

When Allah's words, spoken to Muhammad, were written down, they became the Qur'an ("that which is recited"). The Qur'an (or Koran) is the holy book of the Islamic faith. It is divided into 114 *suras* (chapters), containing about 77,700 words, and teaches that Allah is the only god, who demands submission from humankind.

A page from the Qur'an, written in Arabic. Its words are those of Allah, as revealed to the Prophet Muhammad.

The name of the Prophet Muhammad, written in Arabic script.

Start of the Islamic Era

In Mecca, Arabia, Muhammad was persecuted for his belief that Allah was the only god. In 622, he and his followers were invited to Yathrib, 200 miles (320 km) to the north. Their migration (*hijra* in Arabic) to this friendly city, now known as Medina, marks the start of the Islamic era. The Islamic calendar dates from this time, so the year 622 of the Christian calendar is counted as year 1 of the Islamic calendar.

ISLAM
c. 570 *Birth of Muhammad.*
613 *Muhammad begins to preach in Mecca, Arabia.*
622 *Muhammad moves to Medina; Islam begins.*
624–628 *War with Mecca.*
632 *Muhammad dies.*
670 *Islam spreads to northwest Africa.*
711 *Islam spreads to Europe (Spain).*
733 *Battle of Tours, France, halts spread of Islam in Europe.*
800s–900s *Islamic states emerge (Iraq, Iran, Egypt, Syria, Afghanistan).*

The landscape of Medina ("City of the Prophet") in the time of Muhammad may have looked like this, situated on a fertile oasis.

Islamic Art

Islamic art is not religious, unlike Christian art. It seeks to reveal the beauty of objects and buildings through the use of decoration. Books, plates, vases, tiles, floors, walls, and domes are decorated with geometric patterns, and with precisely drawn Arabic letters.

Circular patterns are a common theme in Islamic art. The circle represents infinity, reminding Muslims that Allah is infinite.

The Dome of the Rock, in Jerusalem, was built in 688–691. For Muslims, it is the site of the Prophet Muhammad's ascension to heaven from the rock es-Sakhra. The dome covers the rock.

An open hand is used as a symbol for the Five Pillars of Islam—the essential duties of a Muslim.

In 836, the Abbasid caliphs moved their capital from Baghdad to Samarra, in present-day Iraq. This spiral minaret is from The Great Mosque at Samarra.

The Spread of Islam

slam appealed to people because of its simplicity—Allah was the only god to believe in, and his exact words, as revealed to Muhammad, were written in the Qur'an for every Muslim to read. The new religion was quickly accepted, and within a few years of Muhammad's death it had spread across a vast area, bringing it into conflict with the Christians of Europe.

The Saracens

Islam made its way to northern Africa and parts of Spain in the 7th century thanks to Muslim Arabs from the Arabian peninsula called Saracens. Later, in the 9th century they captured Sicily from the Byzantine Empire and established themselves in parts of southern Italy, Sardinia, Corsica, and southern Gaul. The term "Saracen" was used in the Middle Ages to describe all Muslims, whether they were Arabs, Moors, or Seljuk Turks.

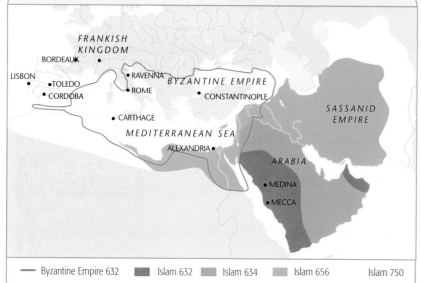

The island of Sicily was invaded by Saracens from North Africa in 827.

CONQUESTS OF ISLAM

FRANKISH KINGDOM
BORDEAUX
LISBON
TOLEDO
CORDOBA
RAVENNA
ROME
BYZANTINE EMPIRE
CONSTANTINOPLE
CARTHAGE
SASSANID EMPIRE
MEDITERRANEAN SEA
ALEXANDRIA
ARABIA
MEDINA
MECCA

— Byzantine Empire 632 ■ Islam 632 Islam 634 Islam 656 Islam 750

The Growth of an Empire
The successors of Muhammad (the caliphs) embarked on a series of conquests. By 661, Muslim armies had taken Iraq, Iran, Palestine, Syria, and Egypt. Further gains brought Afghanistan and North Africa under Arab control, and in 711 a Muslim army invaded Spain. The Islamic empire stretched from the Atlantic to the borders of China.

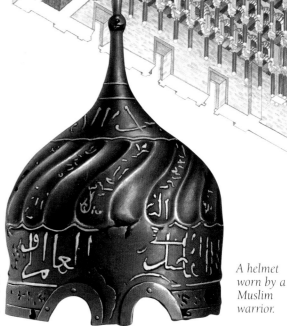

Muhammad's Successors
Muhammad died in 632 and his father-in-law Abu Bakr (c. 573–634) became ruler of the Islamic world. He was the first caliph, from the Arabic word *khalifa*, meaning "successor to the Prophet." In 661, power passed to the Umayyad family, whose caliphs ruled the Islamic empire from Damascus, Syria. In 750, the Abbasid family overthrew the Umayyads, and their caliphs ruled from Baghdad, Iraq, for almost 500 years.

A helmet worn by a Muslim warrior.

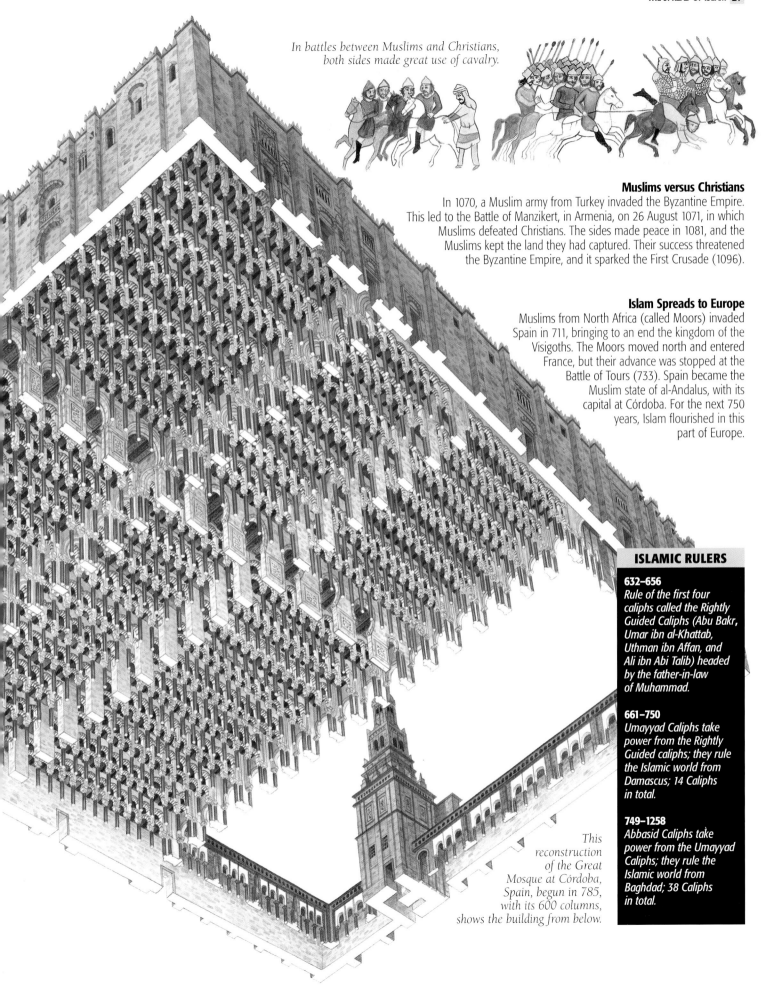

In battles between Muslims and Christians, both sides made great use of cavalry.

Muslims versus Christians

In 1070, a Muslim army from Turkey invaded the Byzantine Empire. This led to the Battle of Manzikert, in Armenia, on 26 August 1071, in which Muslims defeated Christians. The sides made peace in 1081, and the Muslims kept the land they had captured. Their success threatened the Byzantine Empire, and it sparked the First Crusade (1096).

Islam Spreads to Europe

Muslims from North Africa (called Moors) invaded Spain in 711, bringing to an end the kingdom of the Visigoths. The Moors moved north and entered France, but their advance was stopped at the Battle of Tours (733). Spain became the Muslim state of al-Andalus, with its capital at Córdoba. For the next 750 years, Islam flourished in this part of Europe.

This reconstruction of the Great Mosque at Córdoba, Spain, begun in 785, with its 600 columns, shows the building from below.

ISLAMIC RULERS

632–656
Rule of the first four caliphs called the Rightly Guided Caliphs (Abu Bakr, Umar ibn al-Khattab, Uthman ibn Affan, and Ali ibn Abi Talib) headed by the father-in-law of Muhammad.

661–750
Umayyad Caliphs take power from the Rightly Guided caliphs; they rule the Islamic world from Damascus; 14 Caliphs in total.

749–1258
Abbasid Caliphs take power from the Umayyad Caliphs; they rule the Islamic world from Baghdad; 38 Caliphs in total.

An axe-hammer dating from the early 500s—a typical weapon of a Germanic warrior. It was used in close combat, and as a throwing weapon.

The Franks

The Franks were one of the most warlike of the Germanic groups. Their warriors were armed with heavy throwing weapons that they hurled as they charged. Their most famous weapon was the francisca, which was a throwing axe. The Franks were perhaps named after this axe, which could be thrown over a range of about 50 feet (15 m).

A Revolutionary Device

The stirrup revolutionized Medieval warfare. It gave support to riders, and allowed them to control their horses better. Soldiers stood up in their stirrups to throw spears, and could sit back in their saddles to shoot arrows.

A stirrup is a ring with a flat bottom, usually hung from each side of a saddle to create a footrest for the rider on a horse. This stirrup, from England, was made in the 11th century.

The Viking Warriors

For 300 years, between the 790s and 1090s, Vikings from Norway, Sweden, and Denmark raided northern and southern Europe, Britain, and Ireland. They attacked and looted monasteries, towns, and villages. They also took slaves, whom they traded with Arab merchants in exchange for silver. Viking warriors fought with double-edged swords, axes, spears, and bows and arrows. They defended themselves with shields, and body armor made from leather or metal chainmail.

A Viking warrior armed with his battle-axe and sword. For protection the Vikings wore chainmail shirts and helmets with nose coverings. They also used wooden shields.

Vikings shot arrows and threw spears at their enemies at the start of a battle.

Weapons and Warfare

Wars were fought throughout the Early Middle Ages. Fighting broke out as one group tried to take control of another's land and possessions. Each side had its own style of weapons and fighting. Some preferred to fight hand-to-hand, whereas others used long-range weapons. It was a time of innovation in equipment and tactics. The introduction of the Arabian horse, a superior breed, and the stirrup, brought major breakthroughs in cavalry tactics.

The Byzantine War Machine

By the 10th century the Byzantine army had become the best-organized and best-equipped fighting force in the Medieval world. The army used battle tactics described in military manuals. At its peak it was a force of around 120,000 men, some of whom were mercenaries—foreigners who were paid to fight for the Byzantines. The elite mercenaries were the Varangian Guard. They were Vikings who were recruited for their fighting strength and skills, and were paid in gold.

A Byzantine commander in his battle armor. When Byzantine troops attacked a stronghold, they climbed its walls with scaling ladders, catapulted rocks, and used battering rams.

Skilled Muslim Archers

Muslim armies made great use of the horse archer—light cavalry armed with powerful bows that shot arrows some 230 feet (70 m). These troops were highly mobile, often making surprise attacks. In battle, horse archers charged at an enemy, then turned away. Thinking the Muslims were retreating the enemy gave chase. The Muslim archers then turned in their saddles and shot back with their arrows. This tactic helped them to win battles against European armies.

The Byzantine Secret Weapon

In 674, Constantinople was besieged by an Arab army from Damascus, Syria. Enemy ships blockaded the harbor, but the Byzantines destroyed them with their secret weapon, known as "Greek Fire." This was a burning mixture of sulphur, resin, and petroleum, squirted through a tube like liquid fire, or hurled in containers from catapults. This weapon was also used to fight off the Vikings in 941.

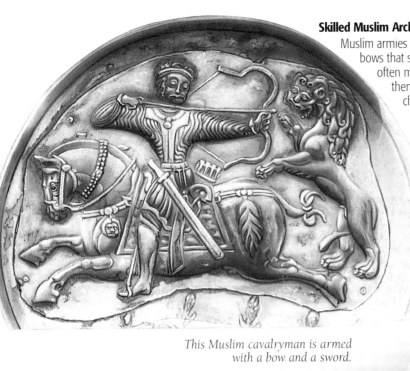

This Muslim cavalryman is armed with a bow and a sword.

A Byzantine flamethrower in action against a Viking ship. Because the burning liquid was oil-based, it floated on the surface of the sea, setting fire to ships' hulls.

Raiders from the North

The wooden stern post, or prow, of a Viking longship was often highly decorated. The animal head carved on this post may have been to frighten an enemy, as well as to let them know the Vikings thought of themselves as fierce warriors.

The Scandinavian countries of Norway, Sweden, and Denmark were the homelands of the Norse, or Vikings. These people were raiders, settlers, and traders, and they had a great influence on northern Europe between 700 and 1100 —a time now known as the Viking Age. At first they struck fear into the communities they raided, but later they became settlers and blended in with the people they had once attacked.

Made from a whale's shoulder bone, this plaque was a Viking smoothing board. A piece of linen was stretched across it, then smoothed until flat.

A berserker, carved as a chess piece, bites his shield in fury. The English word "berserk" (to go into a rage) comes from the Norse.

Women in Viking society

Women had a higher status in Viking society than elsewhere in Europe. For example, a married Viking woman could own land and other property, and she had the right to divorce her husband if the marriage was not a success. Women in other societies did not have these rights. Viking women were in charge of their homes, raising children, cooking, making bread, brewing ale, and making clothes.

Shield-Biting Furious Vikings

Some Viking warriors were known as "berserkers" (bear shirts). Before battle, they dressed in bearskin cloaks and worked themselves up into a rage, howling and biting their shields. They believed their god Odin would make them as strong as bears. Berserkers fought without armor, and did not fear being wounded.

The Raid on Lindisfarne Island

On 7 June 793, Vikings from west Norway raided the Anglo-Saxon monastery on Lindisfarne Island, off the northeast coast of England. The Vikings looted the church, stealing valuables and wrecking altars and holy relics. Some monks were killed and others were taken captive, but it is not known what became of them. This is one of the earliest datable Viking raids, and was in the first wave of raids against Britain, Ireland, and northern Europe.

Armed Viking raiders come ashore from their longships. Defenceless monks are cut down, and the looting and destruction of their property begins.

The Vikings in France

The first Viking raid against the land of the Franks (present-day France, Belgium, Holland, and western Germany) was in 799. Charlemagne, king of the Franks, reacted by strengthening coastal defences. Raiding intensified after his death (814), and the Vikings built a base inside Frankish territory. They sailed along rivers to attack towns, but resistance grew and by the early 1000s the raids had stopped.

The Vikings in Britain and Ireland

The Viking Age in England began in the 780s, and in Scotland and Ireland in the 790s. This was when the Norse raids started. At first, they were small-scale landings, but in the 830s large fleets arrived. England was invaded and divided in two. The Vikings held north and east England, with their capital at Jorvik (York), while the Anglo-Saxons kept the south.

This copper-plated and red-enameled casket, once used as a reliquary by Scottish monks, was taken by Viking raiders as loot.

Funerary stones from Gotland, like the one shown here, reveal many aspects of Viking everyday life and beliefs.

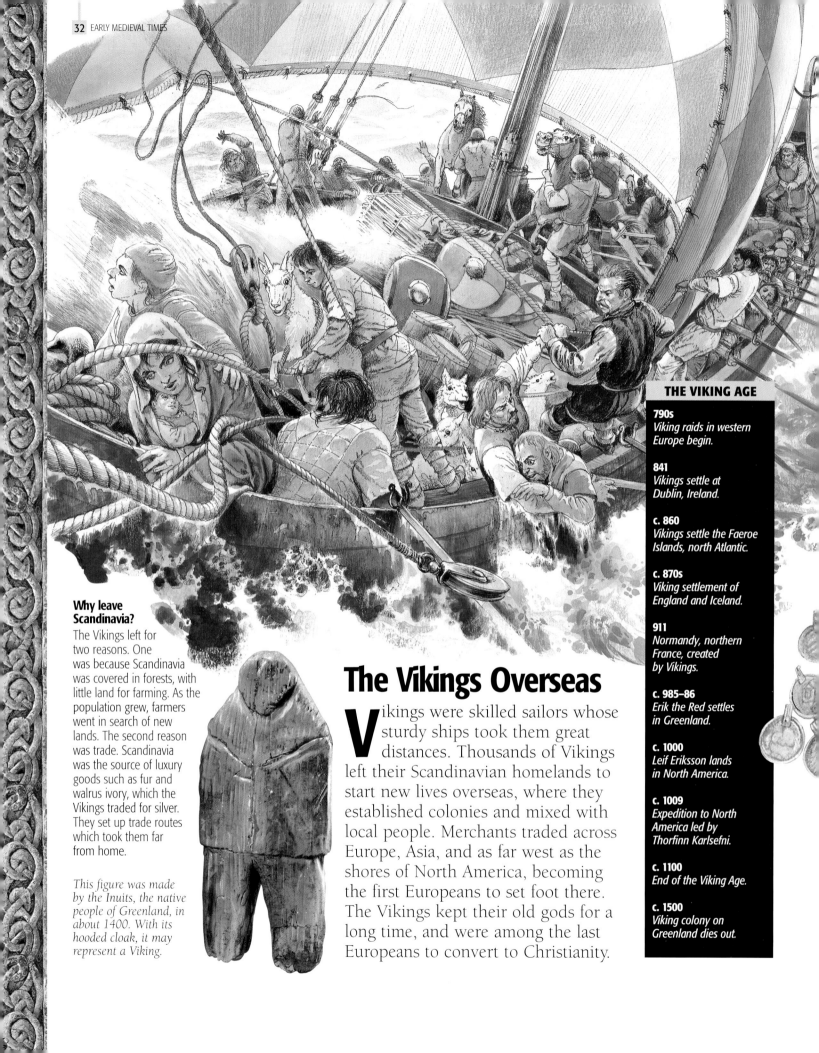

Why leave Scandinavia?

The Vikings left for two reasons. One was because Scandinavia was covered in forests, with little land for farming. As the population grew, farmers went in search of new lands. The second reason was trade. Scandinavia was the source of luxury goods such as fur and walrus ivory, which the Vikings traded for silver. They set up trade routes which took them far from home.

This figure was made by the Inuits, the native people of Greenland, in about 1400. With its hooded cloak, it may represent a Viking.

The Vikings Overseas

Vikings were skilled sailors whose sturdy ships took them great distances. Thousands of Vikings left their Scandinavian homelands to start new lives overseas, where they established colonies and mixed with local people. Merchants traded across Europe, Asia, and as far west as the shores of North America, becoming the first Europeans to set foot there. The Vikings kept their old gods for a long time, and were among the last Europeans to convert to Christianity.

THE VIKING AGE

790s
Viking raids in western Europe begin.

841
Vikings settle at Dublin, Ireland.

c. 860
Vikings settle the Faeroe Islands, north Atlantic.

c. 870s
Viking settlement of England and Iceland.

911
Normandy, northern France, created by Vikings.

c. 985–86
Erik the Red settles in Greenland.

c. 1000
Leif Eriksson lands in North America.

c. 1009
Expedition to North America led by Thorfinn Karlsefni.

c. 1100
End of the Viking Age.

c. 1500
Viking colony on Greenland dies out.

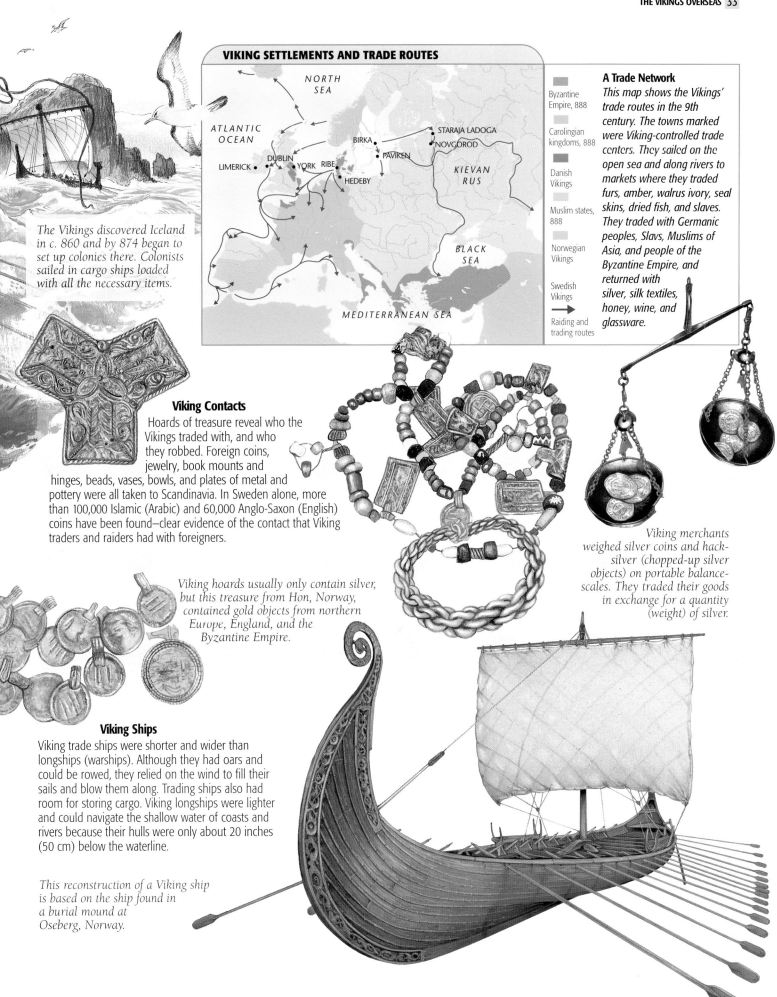

VIKING SETTLEMENTS AND TRADE ROUTES

NORTH SEA

ATLANTIC OCEAN

LIMERICK   DUBLIN   YORK   RIBE
BIRKA   STARAJA LADOGA
NOVGOROD
PAVIKEN
HEDEBY
KIEVAN RUS
BLACK SEA
MEDITERRANEAN SEA

Byzantine Empire, 888

Carolingian kingdoms, 888

Danish Vikings

Muslim states, 888

Norwegian Vikings

Swedish Vikings

→ Raiding and trading routes

A Trade Network

This map shows the Vikings' trade routes in the 9th century. The towns marked were Viking-controlled trade centers. They sailed on the open sea and along rivers to markets where they traded furs, amber, walrus ivory, seal skins, dried fish, and slaves. They traded with Germanic peoples, Slavs, Muslims of Asia, and people of the Byzantine Empire, and returned with silver, silk textiles, honey, wine, and glassware.

The Vikings discovered Iceland in c. 860 and by 874 began to set up colonies there. Colonists sailed in cargo ships loaded with all the necessary items.

Viking Contacts

Hoards of treasure reveal who the Vikings traded with, and who they robbed. Foreign coins, jewelry, book mounts and hinges, beads, vases, bowls, and plates of metal and pottery were all taken to Scandinavia. In Sweden alone, more than 100,000 Islamic (Arabic) and 60,000 Anglo-Saxon (English) coins have been found—clear evidence of the contact that Viking traders and raiders had with foreigners.

Viking hoards usually only contain silver, but this treasure from Hon, Norway, contained gold objects from northern Europe, England, and the Byzantine Empire.

Viking merchants weighed silver coins and hack-silver (chopped-up silver objects) on portable balance-scales. They traded their goods in exchange for a quantity (weight) of silver.

Viking Ships

Viking trade ships were shorter and wider than longships (warships). Although they had oars and could be rowed, they relied on the wind to fill their sails and blow them along. Trading ships also had room for storing cargo. Viking longships were lighter and could navigate the shallow water of coasts and rivers because their hulls were only about 20 inches (50 cm) below the waterline.

This reconstruction of a Viking ship is based on the ship found in a burial mound at Oseberg, Norway.

The Birth of Russia

Russia was created in the 800s, when Vikings from Sweden, known as the "Rus," began to settle in eastern Europe. They traded with the local population of Slavs, took control of Slav towns, and by the late 860s had built a Rus state, which came to be known as "Russia." It grew into a large and important region, with close links to the Byzantine Empire and the Eastern Church.

An amber and glass bead necklace. Amber, an orange-colored fossilized tree resin, was traded by Vikings throughout early Russia.

This silver dress pin in the shape of a dragon's head was found in a Viking grave at an early settlement site in Russia.

Following Vladimir's conversion to Christianity, he ordered the building of the Church of the Tithe, Kiev. Constructed between 989 and 996 by craftsmen from the Byzantine Empire, it was the first stone church in Russia.

RUSSIA

862
Rurik, legendary warrior, supposedly gains control of Novgorod and founds the princely dynasty of Kievan Rus.

882
Oleg gains control of Kiev, the future capital.

c. 890
The Cyrillic alphabet is created in Bulgaria.

988
Grand Duke Vladimir I becomes an Eastern Orthodox Christian.

996
The Church of the Tithe is built.

1019–1054
Yaroslav the Wise (978–1054), son of Vladimir I, is grand duke of Kiev.

1037
St. Sophia Cathedral in Kiev, named after the great cathedral of St. Sophia, Constantinople, is founded.

Here, Slavs offer furs to a Rus, who is probably a trader.

Vikings Known as the Rus
From c. 750 Vikings from Sweden crossed into eastern Europe. They originally entered Slav territory as traders, sailing along the great rivers and collecting furs for sale in the west. Their travels took them as far as Constantinople, capital of the Byzantine Empire, before they settled permanently in eastern Europe and along the banks of the Volga River in present-day Russia.

The Slavs
The original inhabitants of eastern and central Europe were groups of peoples known as Slavs. They were warlike, and built fortresses to defend their territory. The Rus traded with the Slavs, and eventually settled in their towns and mixed with them. Slavs taught the Rus how to build bridges— and the Rus taught them shipbuilding.

EXPANSION OF THE RUS

BALTIC SEA • NOVGOROD • PSKOV KIEVAN RUS VIATCHIANS POLES DEREVLIANS SEVERYANS • PRAGUE KIEV BOHEMIANS SLOVAKS MAGYARS MORAVIANS SERBS BLACK SEA

— Kievan Rus, c. 1050 ▨ Temporary gain by Germany, 929–982 ▨ Slavic peoples

The First Russian State
When the Rus began to settle in eastern Europe, they lived in towns such as Novgorod and Kiev. These towns belonged to people known as Slavs, but in the 800s the Rus took control of them. From these towns, the Rus were able to command the surrounding countryside. By the 860s, Novgorod had become the capital of a Rus state, with Rurik its first leader. By the 950s the Rus controlled a large part of eastern Europe.

Translating the Bible
Methodius (c. 825–885) and his brother Cyril (c. 827–869) were Greeks who spoke Slavonic. They became priests, and in 863 were sent by the Eastern Church to the Slavs. They translated the Bible into the Slavonic language and invented the first Slavonic alphabet, called Glagolitic, so that the scriptures could be written down. After they died, Methodius and Cyril were made saints.

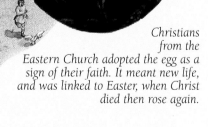

Christians from the Eastern Church adopted the egg as a sign of their faith. It meant new life, and was linked to Easter, when Christ died then rose again.

The alphabet named after St. Cyril, called Cyrillic, is based on the Greek alphabet. It is used today in parts of eastern Europe, Russia, and by the Eastern Church.

Christianity Reaches Russia
Missionaries from the Eastern Church and the Western Church tried to introduce the Christian faith to pagan Russia. Vladimir I (956–1015), ruler of Kiev, sent officials to look at both styles of Christianity. He decided to follow the Eastern Church (from Constantinople), believing it was purer than the Western Church (from Rome). In 988, Vladimir was baptized, and his people followed his example. From then on, Christianity was the religion of Russia.

EASTERN EUROPE

570s
The Slavs attack the Byzantine Empire.

600s
The Slavs conquer the Balkan region of eastern Europe.

800s
The Great Moravian State flourishes in central Europe.

Late 800s
Magyars (Hungarians) invade central Europe and raid Germany, Italy, and France.

Early 900s
The Great Moravian State collapses due to the Magyar invasion.

955
Germans defeat the Magyars at the Battle of Lechfeld, halting their advance across Europe and forcing them to retreat to Hungary.

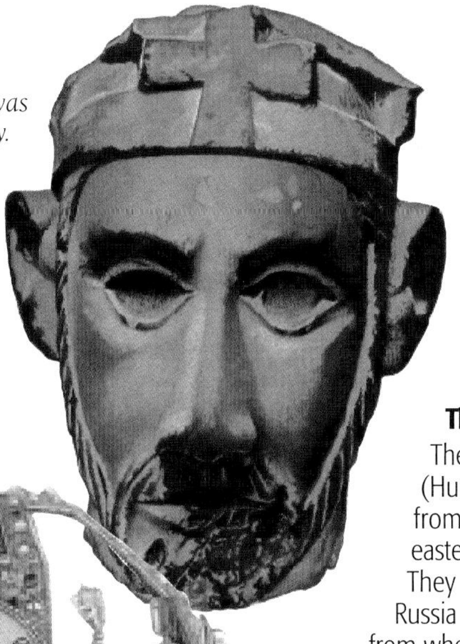

Stephen I (c.975–1038) was the first king of Hungary. He was crowned on Christmas Day 1000, with a gold crown sent by the pope.

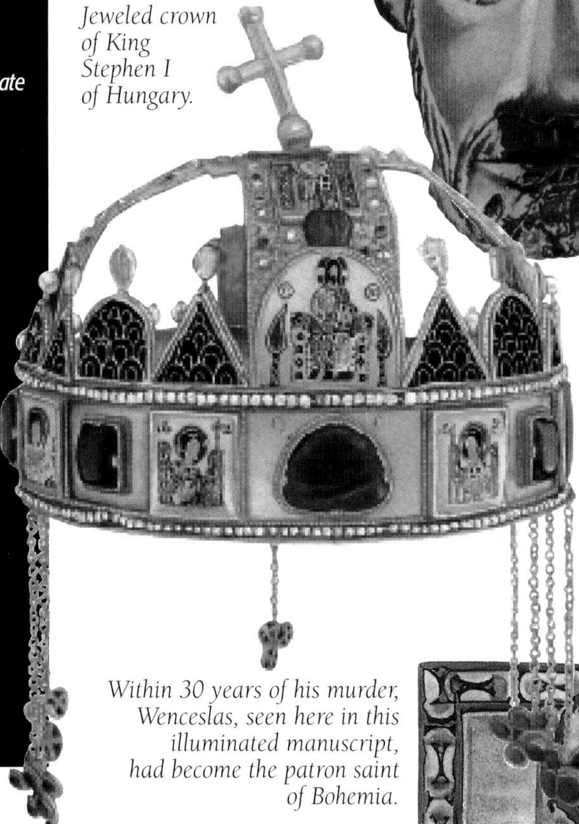

Jeweled crown of King Stephen I of Hungary.

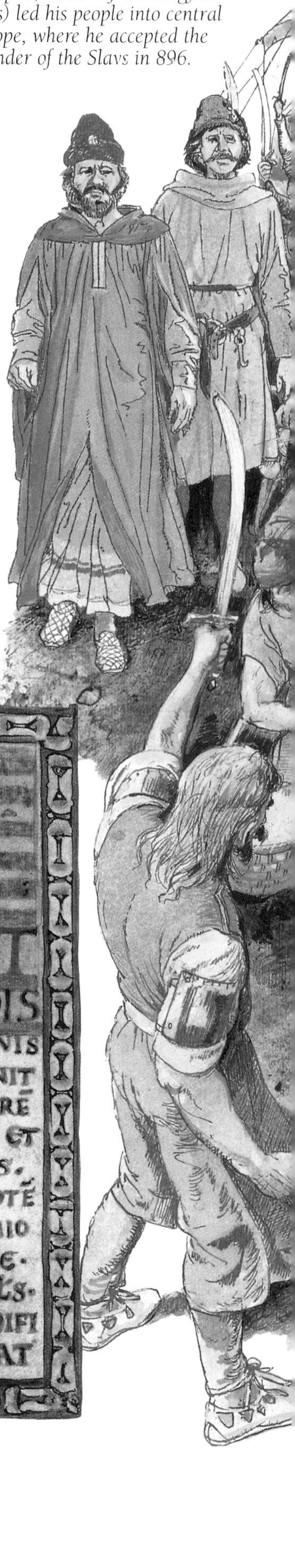

Árpád, leader of the Magyars (Hungarians) led his people into central Europe, where he accepted the surrender of the Slavs in 896.

The Magyars

The Magyars (Hungarians) came from the steppes of eastern Europe. They were settled in Russia by the 830s, from where they moved into what became Hungary. They attacked German territories north and west of Hungary, and successfully invaded northern Italy and France in 954. Following defeat by the Germans in 955, the Magyars retreated east, and made Hungary their home.

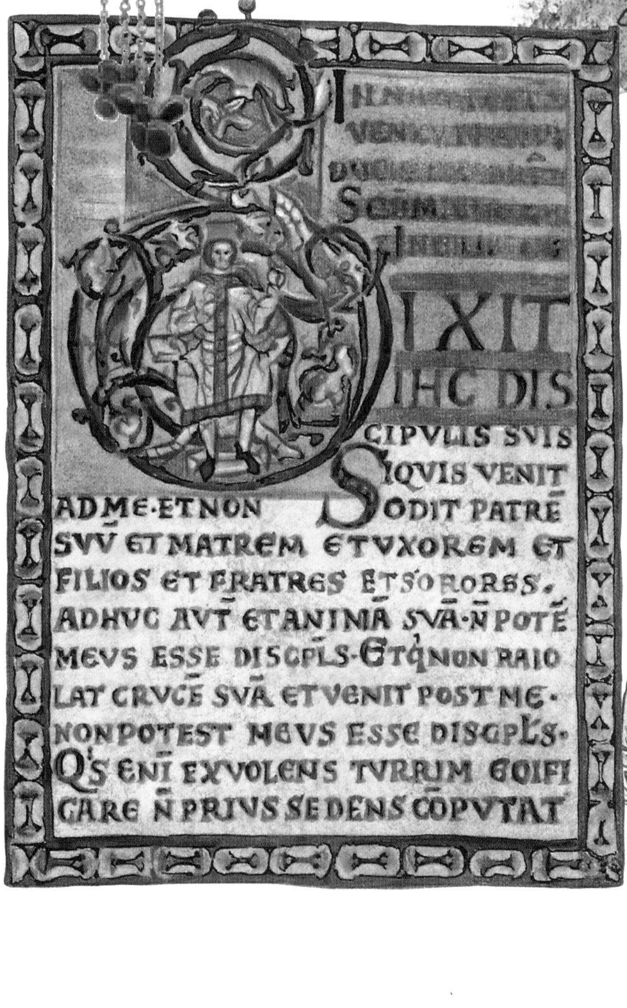

Within 30 years of his murder, Wenceslas, seen here in this illuminated manuscript, had become the patron saint of Bohemia.

The Duke of Bohemia

Wenceslas (907–935) was born in Bohemia. In 922, after becoming Duke of Bohemia, he formed links with neighboring Germany, recognized Henry I of Germany as his king and allowed missionaries to bring Christianity to Bohemia. These acts angered many Bohemian nobles, who murdered Wenceslas.

Eastern Europe

As the Roman Empire broke up in the 400s eastern tribes raided central Europe: first the Huns and later the Avars. By the 600s they were followed by Slav tribes, also from the east. They created kingdoms centered on Bohemia, Moravia, and Slovakia (the present-day Czech Republic), and the short-lived Great Moravian State of the 800s, which was the first Slav empire.

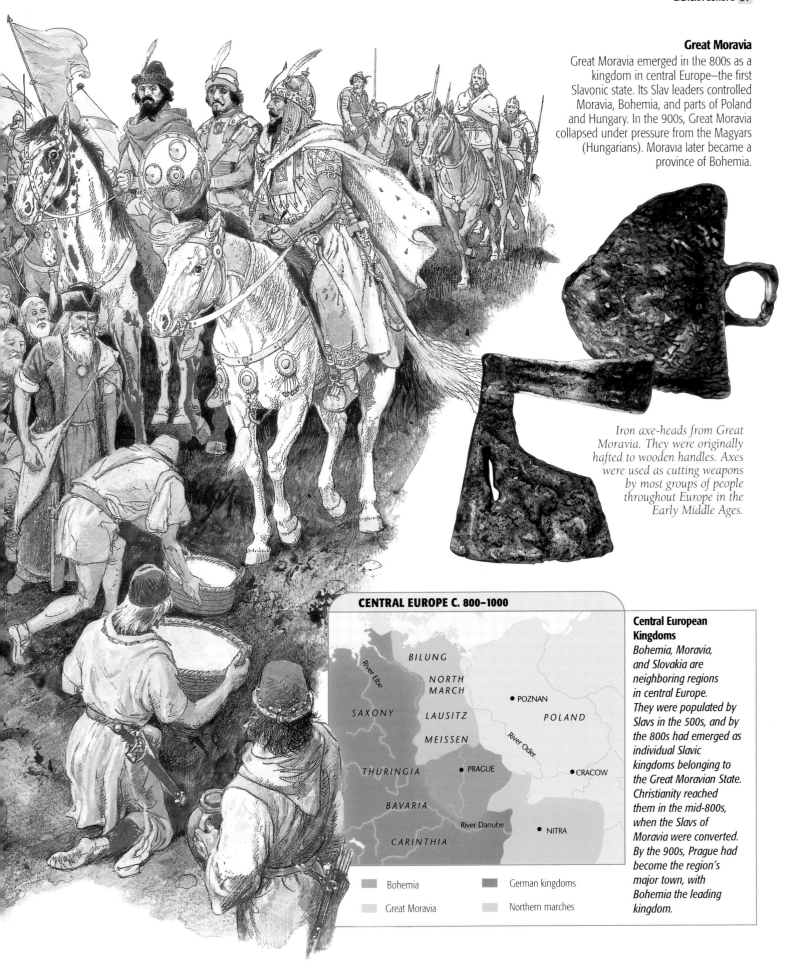

Great Moravia

Great Moravia emerged in the 800s as a kingdom in central Europe—the first Slavonic state. Its Slav leaders controlled Moravia, Bohemia, and parts of Poland and Hungary. In the 900s, Great Moravia collapsed under pressure from the Magyars (Hungarians). Moravia later became a province of Bohemia.

Iron axe-heads from Great Moravia. They were originally hafted to wooden handles. Axes were used as cutting weapons by most groups of people throughout Europe in the Early Middle Ages.

CENTRAL EUROPE C. 800–1000

BILUNG

NORTH MARCH

• POZNAN

SAXONY

LAUSITZ

POLAND

River Elbe

MEISSEN

River Oder

THURINGIA

• PRAGUE

• CRACOW

BAVARIA

River Danube

• NITRA

CARINTHIA

Bohemia

German kingdoms

Great Moravia

Northern marches

Central European Kingdoms

Bohemia, Moravia, and Slovakia are neighboring regions in central Europe. They were populated by Slavs in the 500s, and by the 800s had emerged as individual Slavic kingdoms belonging to the Great Moravian State. Christianity reached them in the mid-800s, when the Slavs of Moravia were converted. By the 900s, Prague had become the region's major town, with Bohemia the leading kingdom.

The Holy Roman Empire and the Church

The Holy Roman Empire, also known as the First German Empire, continues the story of Charlemagne. He forged an empire across Europe. It was intended to recreate the glory of the Roman Empire, with a single leader in charge. It failed, amid family feuding and foreign invasions. However, Charlemagne's vision did not die. It was revived in the 900s by German kings who formed a partnership with the Western Church. This led to a struggle between popes and kings as to who should have overall power.

Despite being outnumbered five to one, the Germans won the Battle of Lechfeld because their cavalry (left) wore better armor than the Magyars (right).

The Battle of Lechfeld

After their raid into France and Italy in 954, the Magyars marched into Germany. In 955, a force of 50,000 Magyars fought 10,000 Germans in the Battle of Lechfeld. It was a German victory. The Magyars fled eastward, never to return.

One of the many things the Western and Eastern churches disagreed about was how the sacrament of Communion (the wine and bread given during mass) was to be administered. This 6th-century Byzantine plate shows Christ giving Communion to his disciples.

Ambassadors from Slavinia (the countries of the Slavs), Germany, France and Italy bow down to Otto III, their emperor and head of the Holy Roman Empire.

This drawing shows the pope (left) and the Holy Roman Emperor (right) sharing the throne. In fact, they saw themselves more as rivals than equals.

The Papal States

In 321, Constantine, the first Christian Roman emperor, passed a law allowing the Church to own land. In the 750s, the Franks gave the pope lands in central Italy, captured from the Lombards. They became the basis of the Papal States (the states of the Church). Through treaties and donations, the Church received more land in central Italy. The pope viewed himself as ruler of the Papal States, but this caused conflict with the German emperors of the Holy Roman Empire who felt they should have overall leadership.

THE HOLY ROMAN EMPIRE AND THE CHURCH

AACHEN (AIX-LA-CHAPELLE)

PARIS

LECHFELD

TOULOUSE

BOLOGNA • RAVENNA

PERUGIA

ROME

MEDITERRANEAN SEA

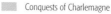

Conquests of Charlemagne	Regions recognizing Charlemagne as overlord	Byzantine possessions
Conquest of Pepin	Frankish kingdoms, 751	Church states, part of Charlemagne's empire

The East-West Schism

Besides the Holy Roman Emperor, the pope faced another obstacle in his struggle for power: the Eastern Orthodox Church. Papal authority was not recognized by the patriarch, the highest-ranking bishop of Constantinople.
In 1054, the Churches denounced each other. Both Pope Leo IX (1002–1054) and the patriarch Michael Cerularius (died 1058) excommunicated each other. This made the schism permanent, and each Church then went its own way.

The Holy Roman Empire

Charlemagne had become the first emperor in the West since the end of the Roman Empire in the 400s. His empire covered much of France, Germany, and a central strip from the North Sea to northern Italy. It was this empire–the Carolingian Empire–that later kings of Germany sought to revive, beginning with Otto I who became emperor in 962. Because it had the support of the pope, it took the name "Holy" Roman Empire. However, because its emperors saw themselves as head of the Church, not just part of it, centuries of bickering followed.

The gold crown of Emperor Otto I, used at his coronation ceremony in 962.

Inside this lancehead was said to be a major holy relic—a piece of the cross on which Christ was crucified. The lance belonged to Emperor Otto I.

Otto III

Otto III (980–1002) became king of Germany at the age of three, and his mother and grandmother acted for him until he came of age in 994. In 996 Otto was crowned Emperor of the Holy Roman Empire (Germany and Italy combined). He wanted to revive the glory of the ancient past, and he made Rome his capital. Otto wanted to be leader of the Christian Church, but his attempt failed and he was forced from Rome, never to return.

Otto III, pictured as Holy Roman Emperor, a title first used by his grandfather, Otto I.

The Islamic World

After the death of Muhammad in 632, a succession of caliphs took charge, ensuring that the word of Allah, as contained in the Qu'ran, spread rapidly. However, disagreements occurred, and Islam divided into two branches. Meanwhile, the arts and sciences flourished, particularly in Baghdad which became a major center of learning. Scholars added to the knowledge of the ancient Greeks, and developed many ideas of their own. Their mathematicians studied numbers, astronomers watched the stars, and geographers made maps. It was an important period of scientific discovery.

Abbasid mosques contained niches called mihrabs *(like the one shown left). They were used for prayer and indicated the direction of Mecca.*

This Fatimid glass bowl, with elegant decoration, may have been hung and used as a lamp.

A Sufi musician with a tambourine. Music is important in Sufi ceremonies, where a rhythmic tune and chanting helps followers reach a trance-like state and feel close to Allah.

Islamic Law

Muslims believe that Allah gave instructions for how they should live their lives, and what laws they must follow. The sacred law of Islam is known as the *shari'a* ("clear path"). For Muslims, a life of devotion to *shari'a* is essential if they are to enter heaven when they die. *Shari'a* governs every aspect of a Muslim's life, and is the path created for him or her by Allah. Only by leading obedient lives, faithful to *shari'a,* will Allah guide Muslims to heaven.

Sufism: the Mystical Branch of Islam

Sufism is another branch of Islam, separate from Shi'ism and Sunnism. Those who follow it are called Sufis, which means "wearers of wool" (after the woolen clothes worn by early Sufis). The movement was begun by devout Muslims in the late 600s. They were concerned that some Muslims were becoming too materialistic. The early Sufis wanted Muslims to lead simpler lives, and spend more time in prayer.

The Mosque

In the religion of Islam, a mosque is a building used as a place of worship, education, and teaching. The first mosque was built at Medina, Saudi Arabia, in the house where the Prophet Muhammad went to live in 622. All mosques are based on the design of that building, being either square or rectangular. A minaret, or tower, stands at the front, from where Muslims are called to prayer five times a day. Worshipers always face the holy city of Mecca to pray.

A Shi'ite standard with the names of Allah, Muhammad and the caliph Ali.

Shi'ism and Sunnism

In the 660s, Islam divided into two main branches—Shi'ism and Sunnism. Shi'ism (followers are called Shi'ites) took its name from the Shiat Ali, the "party of Ali." Ali (c. 598–660) was the fourth caliph or ruler of Islam, and a cousin of Muhammad. The Shi'ites claimed that only the descendants of Ali could become leaders of Islam. In Sunnism (followers are called Sunnis) the Qur'an is regarded as the ultimate rule of Islam. Sunnism became, and still is, the larger of Islam's two branches.

Baghdad: Center of Islamic Learning

Baghdad, capital of present-day Iraq, was founded in 762. Between the 8th and 12th centuries the city was the center of Islamic education and culture, where Muslim scholars studied medicine, mathematics, astronomy, chemistry, literature and more. They translated and studied the works of ancient Greek scholars, preserving valuable knowledge which the people of Europe had lost following the collapse of the Roman Empire. Baghdad blossomed, and became a city of museums, hospitals, libraries, and mosques.

A page from a book written by Muhammad al-Khwarizmi (c. 800–850), a great Persian mathematician.

At the House of Wisdom, Baghdad, great translation projects took place, converting Greek and Latin books into Arabic. The House of Wisdom was begun in 830.

Society in the First Millennium

I t is historians who label the period from the end of the Western Roman Empire in the late-400s to around the year 1000 the "Early Middle Ages." Those who lived during these 600 years gave it no such name. As we review the period and draw its many strands together, we see how, by the end of the period, the population was rising, the Church was gaining greater influence, and Christian society was beginning to take shape. Many of today's villages began life at this time, and while peasant farmers worked the land, new laws were created to govern the people.

Punishment for crimes in Viking society was severe. Stealing sheep was considered a greater crime than murder. Here an offender is being hanged.

The Fall and Rise of Europe's Population

In 500, Europe's population stood at perhaps 27 million. Then came a sharp decline, brought about by migrations and plague. In 650, the population total may have fallen to as low as 18 million. Thereafter, as the migration of peoples slowed, and living conditions improved, the population increased until, by 1000, it had reached an estimated 38 million.

Law Systems

At first, Germanic law was crude and savage. It was based on tribal customs handed down from one generation to the next. For example, if a person committed murder, the law said his whole family could be punished. This led to family feuds. To prove their innocence, a person might undertake an ordeal, such as being thrown into a pool of holy water. If he floated, the water had rejected him and he was guilty. If he sank, he was innocent, and was pulled out before drowning. These old customs were replaced by a system of fines.

Only wealthy farmers could pay taxes in coins. These coins were made between 1005 and 1025.

Taxes

Just as in modern times, people in early Medieval society paid taxes. Thanks to its taxpayers, the Byzantine Empire became one of the wealthiest empires in the early Medieval period. The most important source of its wealth came from the land tax which was imposed on all villages in the empire. Villagers paid as a single unit. If one villager died, his neighbors were responsible for paying his share of the village tax.

Charlemagne and his wife. Above their heads are the hands of God—the ultimate law-maker.

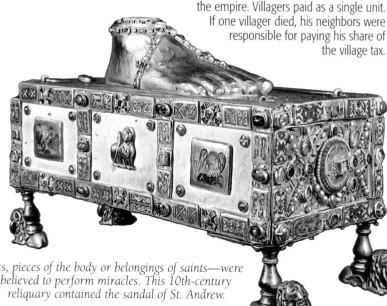

Relics, pieces of the body or belongings of saints—were believed to perform miracles. This 10th-century reliquary contained the sandal of St. Andrew.

Christian Belief

By the year 1000, the conversion of western Europe to Christianity was nearing completion (only the Viking regions of Norway and Sweden remained loyal to their pagan gods). The Church became a major part of people's everyday lives, exerting a powerful grip on their minds. Belief in a good God was balanced by belief in the devil. People lived in fear that for their sins in this life they would be punished by eternal torment in the next.

Panic quickly spread at the dawn of the new millennium. Many people believed that the world would end in the year 1033, the thousandth anniversary of the death of Jesus Christ. This 11th-century illustration depicts an episode of the book of the Apocalypse, a book of the Bible that describes the destruction of the world.

In the Middle Ages, the devil was pictured as a monster who devoured the souls of sinners. These wretches were not worthy to enter the kingdom of Heaven.

Marriage

The classical world (the world of the Romans, and the Greeks before them) began slipping into the past and was being replaced by new ways of thinking and working. However many aspects of society did not change. Marriage in the Medieval period, as in ancient times, marked the passing of the rights over a woman's property from her father to her husband. A women was not recognized as an individual person under the law, but rather as the property of her father or husband. In return for these rights, men were obliged to protect women.

Upheaval in the Medieval World

The world we know today actually started to emerge during the Early Medieval Period. As society was being divided between those with land, and those without, the new millennium brought changes to the Medieval world on a political level as well. The Muslims, who were to become a formidable threat to Christian society in the years to come, laid siege to many lands of the Mediterranean. New nations were founded, while the Normans, a new military power, conquered many lands, bringing a distinct culture to many parts of Europe.

Muslim Threats

Muslim forces posed a serious threat to many Christian lands in the Mediterranean, including the Italian peninsula, the islands, and the Byzantine Empire. In 1004, Arabs occupied Corsica, sacked Pisa, and laid siege to Bari, in southern Italy. In 1015, Genoa and Pisa allied to win back Corsica from the Arabs while Venice came to Bari's rescue. Sardinia was finally freed from Arab forces in 1052 by the Pisans only to be forced under Pisan control for almost three centuries.

This decoration from an ivory casket shows the Arab ruler Abd al-Malik (from 1002 to 1008) and two servants.

Civil War in Spain

The period between 1009 and 1031 was a time of unrest in the Muslim regions of Spain and Portugal. Civil war broke out in the caliphate of Córdoba after the death of the caliph Abd ar-Rahman in 1008. Fighting among Arabs, Berbers, and slaves led to the ultimate partitioning of the caliphate. It was divided into dozens of small, independent kingdoms called *taifas* in 1031. Regional Muslim dynasties ruled cities such as Seville, Granada, Malaga, Toledo, and Zaragoza.

This detail from a Byzantine manuscript illustrating the siege of Thessalonika, northern Greece, shows Muslim invaders carrying off captives as slaves.

Boleslaw the Brave

The state of Poland was founded in 966 when the Piast duke, Mieszko I (c. 963–992), converted to Christianity to avoid a takeover by the Holy Roman Emperor. Upon his death, his son, Boleslaw the Brave, became duke and, in 992, the first king of Poland. Under Boleslaw's reign Polish territory expanded to include Pomerania and Crakow. Further expansions brought him into conflict with Holy Roman Emperor Henry II, who declared war. Fighting continued until 1018, when a treaty granted Boleslaw control of his gains, including parts of Moravia and Bohemia.

This 10th-century silver chalice, possibly of German origin, was found near a monastery in Poland. Decorated with scenes from the Old Testament, it may have been brought over by missionaries after Christianity was adopted in 966.

Detail from the Bayeux Tapestry which shows fighting scenes from the Battle of Hastings.

This detail from the Bayeux Tapestry shows the last Anglo-Saxon king, Harold II (c. 1020–1066), being crowned.

The Normans

The Normans were descendents of the Vikings who settled in northern France in about 900. After establishing the dukedom of Normandy they began their conquest of England, Wales, Scotland, and Ireland as well as southern Italy and Sicily. The Normans, much like their Viking ancestors, were fierce warriors. The most famous Norman victory came in 1066 at the Battle of Hastings, where they defeated the Anglo-Saxons. The duke of Normandy, known as William the Conqueror (c. 1027–1087), became king of England.

Glossary

Alliance A formal agreement between two or more countries, cities, or states, usually for a military purpose.

Baptism A Christian religious ceremony in which someone is bathed or sprinkled with water as a sign that their sin is washed away. They can then become members of the Church.

Burial mound An ancient type of grave raised above ground level. Burial mounds of important people might contain a buried boat or wagon, jewelry and food.

Caliph A spiritual and political leader of Islam. The title was taken by the successors of the Prophet Muhammad in the Islamic world. Their realms were called caliphates.

Cameo A type of round medallion, set into a brooch or a ring, showing the profile of someone's head.

Carolingian The name given to the Frankish dynasty that followed the Merovingians and which ruled from 751 to 987 CE. The dynasty was named after its greatest king, Charlemagne (reigned 768–814 CE).

Casket A small box or chest for valuables, especially jewels. Caskets were prized objects for Vikings in their raids.

Cavalry Soldiers on horseback. Cavalry became important in early Medieval warfare after the invention of the stirrup made it easier to control a horse and wield a weapon at the same time.

Dark Ages An old-fashioned term used to refer to the early Medieval period between the fall of the Roman Empire and the beginning of the second millennium in about 1000, once thought to be an unenlightened period.

Eastern Orthodox Church (Also called the Greek Orthodox Church) The branch of the Church based in the Byzantine Empire that split permanently from the western, Roman Catholic Church in the 11th century.

Excommunicate To expel or to throw someone out of the Church because their beliefs or behavior are contrary to the Church's teachings.

Feud A long and bitter hostility between two people, families, or tribes.

Hermit A religious person who lives alone, usually in the desert, in order to become closer to God. Some of Europe's monastic orders were started by hermits.

Holy relic A part of a saint's body or something that was used by or linked with the saint.

Icon A painted image of Christ, the Virgin Mary, or a saint, sometime worshiped as holy objects. Iconoclasts were people who smashed icons because they thought the Bible prohibited the worship of idols (images or statues of gods).

Illumination In early Medieval times, the skill used by monks to decorate handwritten books with fine illustrations painted in many colors, including gold and silver leaf.

Marches Borders or frontiers, or the land running along them, often in dispute between two tribes or countries.

Medieval Something relating to the Middle Ages.

Merovingian The Frankish dynasty that ruled areas of present-day France, Germany and the Low Countries between c.460 and 751 CE.

Middle Ages A period of history from about the 5th century to the 14th century. The Middle Ages ended when a period called the Renaissance began, when the art and architecture of ancient Greece and Rome were rediscovered.

Millennium The year 1000, the thousandth anniversary of the birth of Christ. It was a common early Medieval belief that Christ would return in that year, or that the world would end in 1033, on the thousandth anniversary of his death.

Minaret The tall thin tower of a mosque. It often has one or more balconies, from which worshipers are called to prayer five times a day.

Mosaic A design or decoration made up of many small pieces of colored glass or stone.

Muscovy A Medieval name for Russia, when the provinces around the capital, Moscow, were ruled by a prince or a duke.

Muslim A follower of Islam. Muslims believe in one God, Allah, and honor the Prophet Muhammad.

Order A religious community of monks or nuns, who often live by strict rules and who take vows to reject worldly things.

Ornate Something that is finely or elaborately decorated.

Pagans People who worshiped pre-Christian gods. The Vikings were the last pagans in western Europe.

Patriarch The head of the Eastern Orthodox Church.

Pope The head of the Roman Catholic Church and the bishop of Rome. From the 10th century onwards, the pope competed with the Holy Roman Emperor for political influence in Europe.

Reliquary A special, ornate container made to house a holy relic.

Saracen A name given to the Arab tribes that attacked the borders of the Roman Empire. Later, the name was used to refer to all Muslim invaders.

Schism The splitting of a group into opposing groups. The split of the Western Church from the Eastern Orthodox Church was called a schism.

Shia A branch of the Muslim faith. Shia Muslims are guided by imams (holy leaders) who are descended from Ali, the Prophet's son-in-law.

Sunni A branch of the Muslim faith. Sunni Muslims follow the example set by the Prophet Muhammad. The majority of Muslims are Sunni.

Tapestry A detailed work of embroidery. The Bayeux tapestry is 231 feet (70 m) long and uses pictures to tell the story of the Norman conquest of England in 1066. The tapestry is a valuable source of historical information.

Thor's hammer The tool used by the Germanic god of thunder to terrify his enemies with thunderbolts. Thor was worshiped by all Germanic peoples in pre-Christian times. Tiny versions of the hammer were worn by people around their necks for protection.

Treaty An official agreeement between two countries, such as over trading rights or borders.

Index